Praise for

UNTANGLE YOUR EMOTIONS

"For anyone who has been taught anything unhelpful or even harmful when it comes to feeling your feelings, this book is your space to heal. My friend Jennie will help you stop simply existing and start really living as you learn how your emotions can help you reconnect with your creator and yourself."

—LYSA TERKEURST, #1 *New York Times* bestselling author and president of Proverbs 31 Ministries

"Notice. Name. Feel. Share. Choose. You'll carry this simple framework with you for the rest of your life. Jennie Allen's ability to integrate the best learnings of psychology with the beautiful vision of Christian spirituality enables us to go far beyond 'feeling our feelings.' You'll learn how our feelings were designed for connection—with God, others, and our own soul—the very connections we all crave. It's time to stop running away; the emotions we fear are the pathway to the healthy soul we all desire."

—JOHN MARK COMER, *New York Times* bestselling author of *Practicing the Way*

"*Untangle Your Emotions* is an accessible biblical guide for anyone struggling to understand emotions, whether their own or those of others. You won't learn how to just manage emotions but how to fully feel—and how the emotions first found in God bless us, bless others, and build up His church."

—PHYLICIA MASONHEIMER, founder and
CEO of Every Woman a Theologian

"We humans are emotion-regulation creatures. For indeed, emotion is the fuel in the tank that enables us to do anything we do. Our trouble, of course, is that we are unfamiliar with our emotions and their God-inspired purposes and functions, and thereby suffer in innumerable ways. Into this trouble Jennie Allen wades with vulnerability, warmth, and practical wisdom. With *Untangle Your Emotions,* she offers us a trustworthy road map that will enable us to more truly partner with God as He forms us into the people of beauty and goodness that He longs for us to become."

—CURT THOMPSON, MD, psychiatrist and author of
The Deepest Place and *The Soul of Shame*

"Jennie Allen is answering one of the biggest questions that people have today: *What do I do with these feelings?!* She is an incredible guide to help you understand where your emotions come from, what to do with them, and how to honor God in processing all that you feel. So many people are going to experience deep healing and gain much needed clarity from the pages ahead! This book is worth thousands of hours of counseling."

—JONATHAN POKLUDA, lead pastor of Harris Creek
Baptist Church, bestselling author, and host of the
Becoming Something podcast

UNTANGLE YOUR EMOTIONS

UNTANGLE YOUR EMOTIONS

NAMING WHAT YOU FEEL AND
KNOWING WHAT TO DO ABOUT IT

Jennie Allen

WATERBROOK

All Scripture quotations, unless otherwise indicated, are taken from the ESV® Bible (the Holy Bible, English Standard Version®), copyright © 2001 by Crossway, a publishing ministry of Good News Publishers. Used by permission. All rights reserved. Scripture quotations marked (KJV) are taken from the King James Version. Scripture quotations marked (NASB) are taken from the (NASB®) New American Standard Bible®, copyright © 1960, 1971, 1977, 1995, 2020 by the Lockman Foundation. Used by permission. All rights reserved. (www.lockman.org). Scripture quotations marked (NIV) are taken from the Holy Bible, New International Version®, NIV®. Copyright © 1973, 1978, 1984, 2011 by Biblica Inc.® Used by permission. All rights reserved worldwide. Scripture quotations marked (NKJV) are taken from the New King James Version®. Copyright © 1982 by Thomas Nelson. Used by permission. All rights reserved.

Details in some anecdotes and stories have been changed to protect the identities of the persons involved.

Published in the United States by WaterBrook, an imprint of Random House, a division of Penguin Random House LLC.

WATERBROOK and colophon are registered trademarks of Penguin Random House LLC.

Published in association with Yates & Yates, www.yates2.com.

Hardback ISBN 978-0-593-19341-9
Ebook ISBN 978-0-593-19342-6

The Library of Congress catalog record is available at https://lccn.loc.gov/2023035958.

Printed in the United States of America on acid-free paper.

waterbrookmultnomah.com

9 8 7 6 5 4 3 2 1

FIRST EDITION

Most WaterBrook books are available at special quantity discounts for bulk purchase for premiums, fundraising, and corporate and educational needs by organizations, churches, and businesses. Special books or book excerpts also can be created to fit specific needs. For details, contact specialmarketscms@penguinrandomhouse.com.

Two years ago, I found my way to a
small group committed to living wholeheartedly.
They helped me find my feelings again.

Thanks for never leaving the room, Jess, Linds,
James, Mel, Annie, Toni, and Dr. C.
These words were written, lived, and felt deeply
because of Jesus through you in my life.

I will give you a new heart, and a new spirit I will put within you. And I will remove the heart of stone from your flesh and give you a heart of flesh.

—Ezekiel 36:26

God, we want our hearts to be whole, living, beating, feeling, full, connected to You and to one another. Help.

CONTENTS

PART FOUR
feeling our way forward

we're a bit of a mess

1

WHERE DID *THAT* COME FROM?

This past year, our oldest daughter, Kate, got married, and truly, everything about that day was dreamy: The weather was gorgeous, the venue was idyllic, and everywhere I turned I saw faces belonging to our most beloved people. It was spectacular, every bit of it. My husband, Zac, and I love our son-in-law, Charlie, and we approve wholeheartedly of this match. So much expectation. So much gratitude. So much *joy.*

And then, post-wedding, my heart was pretty quickly wrecked.

For all the good that a child's wedding brings, there is bad that nobody warns you about. Because the moment Kate left our nuclear family—the one made up of Zac and me and her brothers and sister—she and Charlie became their own little family of two.

The *audacity.*

It gets worse.

Kate and Charlie started telling Zac and me about ridiculous dreams they were dreaming, like most people in their twenties, using words like *adventure* and *travel* and *fun*—all words I said to my mom and dad what feels like not so long ago. Over dinner one night, my daughter had the dang nerve to look at her father and me and, with all the casualness in the world, say some stupid sentence that included a whole bunch of words I didn't really hear and three phrases I totally did: "out of the state" . . . "maybe out of the country" . . . "not forever, of course, but for a few years."

Wait. *What?*

A season? Of adventure?

A season of adventure apart from me?

The walls of the room in which we were eating began closing in. My chest, which moments before had felt rightsized for my body, was now two sizes too small for my heart to take a beat. My airways constricted. What fresh hell had I tumbled headlong into? My reaction was not rational, I knew. I realized it in my head, but something bigger than knowing the right answers was happening to me.

I played it cool. I pasted a grin onto my face. I held eye contact with my child—*Nice and steady, Jennie. That's it, that's it*—and I focused on inhaling calmly. This wasn't about me, and I knew it. Equally true: *This was absolutely all about me.*

Thankfully, I didn't erupt that night. I didn't come apart in waves of tears. I didn't faint or fume or fall apart. I made it through in one piece. But the following week, and the week after that and the week after that, in casual conversations with Kate, the subject kept coming up. And again, my chest and airways told me that this wasn't nothing. No, no: This, I knew, was a *thing*.

Cognitively, I understood that I wanted Kate and Charlie to go and create and live their own beautiful story, whatever that meant. So why couldn't my body and heart catch up?

CAN'T STOP THE FEELING

Let me ask you a question: Have you ever had a disproportionate emotional response to a situation that should not have affected you in such a dramatic way?

Let me ask you one more: Have you ever stopped to think about what the reason for that response could be?

There are always things beneath the things. We are not simple creatures. Even those of us determined to live steady, unemotionally charged lives are shaped by a million small moments that stay with us. Those moments shape who we are and how we think and how we react—and, yes, how we feel—in a given moment to a given circumstance.

Among the many things I've been learning and want to share with you in the pages to come is that those revved-up reactions tell a story—a story about something we've lived. They point to a deep-seated something that has gone unaddressed in our heart.

We experience something impactful. We react to that thing by stuffing our feelings or minimizing our feelings or ignoring how we feel altogether. Then something else comes our way, something that's not even that big of a deal, and we lose it. We unload on a loved one. We catastrophize. We ugly cry, heaving until we can barely breathe.

And then we regret what we've done.

Why did we freak out?

Why did we demean our spouse?

Why did we shame our kid or yell at our roommate?

Why did we make that insane assumption and blame and threaten and walk right out the door, slamming it behind us as we left?

What was that all about? What was underneath it all?

Short answer: a *lot,* as the science and the Bible will show us.

Somewhere along the way, maybe from things I heard at church or just from growing up, I learned I wasn't supposed to be sad or angry or scared. I was supposed to be okay, so I needed you to be okay too. Or maybe it's just because I hate the feeling of being out of control, and I believed these feelings were too scary, and sitting in the hard felt . . . too hard.

Every time I experience sadness, fear, anger—emotions I've been conditioned to not want to feel—my brain immediately moves to fight off the feeling, much like my immune system takes down a virus. My brain attacks the feeling, judges it, condemns it, and tells me why I shouldn't feel it at all. It tells me that it is all going to be okay. It barks out all these orders about what I need to do so that I can finally stop feeling the feeling.

Worse still, sometimes when you share with me your sadness, fear, or anger, I do the same stupid thing to you.

I'm sorry.

It's wrong, and I'm sorry. **Your feelings, my feelings, are not evil things that need to be beat back.**

Feelings can't be beat back, by the way. Even if you're the most effective stuffer ever to live, the very best at stuffing feelings way down deep, so far down you believe they can never be found, I'm here to tell you those feelings don't go quietly. The people who know you know that they're there. If you are honest, you know they're there too.

That hint of rage you felt toward your dad, the fear of rejection you felt with your family, the striving that has exhausted you at school or work, the jealousy that creeps in whenever you are at that one friend's house, the bitterness that flickers when you talk about why you don't yet have kids, the despair you feel in your gut

every time you think of the person you love buried under-
ground—I know you think you packed all those things safely
away in a box so that you won't have to see them again.

But inevitably they pop out at unexpected times, like over a
lovely dinner when your daughter is just dreaming beautiful
dreams.

Whatever the triggering situation, at some point the next day
or the next week or sometime even later than that, you look back
on the catalyst—and on your response—thinking, *Why on earth
did I say (or do) that?*

You wonder, *How on earth did those feelings sneak up on me?*
You wonder why they didn't play fair.

The truth of the matter? They *were* playing fair.

Or playing *predictably,* anyway.

Because those feelings are tangled up with something very real
in your past or present, something that absolutely *is* a big deal to
you, whether or not you're ready to admit it.

Feelings can't be beat back.

They can't be ignored or dismissed.

They are trying to tell us something.

THE FEAR BEHIND THE FEAR

I wanted to show up better for Kate, so in that pursuit, I shot
straight with my counselor about what was happening in my
heart and body every time the subject of my daughter leaving
came up. He asked, "Jennie, when did you first experience the
feeling you feel every time Kate talks about moving away?"

My mind flashed to a scene. Have you ever had this happen? I wasn't trying to think of this particular memory, but in one millisecond, there it was, demanding to be seen.

I was standing in the long, cold hospital corridor just outside my husband's room, silently begging God to spare his life, despite some pretty grave reports. "This isn't human," the doctor had said to me after reviewing Zac's blood-pressure results. "Humans can't sustain life with blood pressure this ridiculously high." My husband had suffered a small stroke and was unable to say the right words.

Although eight highly trained, highly pedigreed doctors had gathered around Zac, nobody could determine why his blood pressure continued soaring.

"Please pray"—that's the text I was sending to everyone who cared about us, as I paced those sterile halls.

Please pray.

Please pray.

Please pray.

Weirdly, I held it together emotionally while Zac lay in that hospital bed. Have you ever heard the theory that the reason we go into something of a state of shock whenever crisis hits is so we don't utterly and completely melt down?[1] It's like our brains or our bodies (or a combination of our brains and our bodies) looks at our situation and mutters, "Listen, if we don't all but shut her down, she'll never get out of this alive."

For the days when Zac was stuck inside a hospital, my mind was clear. My memory was sharp. My reflexes were quick. And, miraculously, I didn't crumble under my fears.

But there's a second part to that theory about the protective shock that covers us when crisis initially hits: After about forty-eight hours, that covering disappears. I can vouch for this part of the theory, because on day three, just as Zac was coming home, I completely lost my cool.

Zac's doctors had discharged him not because he had recovered but because, except for a few meds, there was nothing they could do. His blood pressure wasn't yet even close to being within the normal range, but it would take time, they said, and lots of rest. "He's a walking heart attack," one of the doctors had stated with no hint of compassion. "He's got to rest until this BP goes down."

Zac knew this.

I knew this.

Still, we couldn't relax.

How is someone supposed to be *calm* after being given such stressful news?

Rest.

Relax.

Stay calm.

He'd try and try again.

For my part, I felt increasingly consumed by anxiety.

He can't rest.

He can't relax.

He can't stay calm.

I'd lie in bed every night beside my husband, carefully waking nearly every hour so I could lay a hand on his chest, check for a steady heartbeat and the rising of his breath, and exhale relief each time I felt them.

That first hospital stay led to several others, all connected by a sad strand of doctor appointments where Zac was tested, assessed, cautioned, counseled, and medicated further.

"I'm fine," Zac would insist whenever he was asked, even though clearly he wasn't fine.

At some point in this agonizing process, my husband looked at me as if it was finally hitting him and said, "This is pretty serious, I guess."

Um, YES.

You think?

Meanwhile, despite my best attempts to block fear out, it was staking its claim on me.

He's going to stress himself out.

He's going to stress himself out and have a heart attack.

He's going to stress himself out and have a heart attack and leave me all alone.

And there it was: I wasn't afraid simply of Zac's medical condition. I was afraid of losing my best friend. Losing the life I knew. Losing the caretaker of all of us.

I was afraid of being left . . . *alone.*

MY RESPONSE TO my counselor's question—*When did you first experience this feeling?*—was helping me understand that without my being aware of the connection, every time Kate talked about moving away, about leaving me, my brain or heart or soul or whichever part of me holds my feelings was subconsciously zooming back to that first hospital stay and the weeks that followed it, to the time when I was just *sure* I was losing Zac.

Because of my daughter's for-a-season adventures, I'd be abandoned all over again. Something deep inside me believed that not only was I destined to lose Zac very soon, but I would now lose Kate soon too. And Charlie, my new son-in-law. And probably our other three kids—Conner, Caroline, and Cooper—as well. If adulthood meant that one kid left, wouldn't they all?

My subconscious imagination was going all those places as I sat across from Kate at a simple, fun dinner, so I couldn't breathe.

Yep, everyone would leave me.

I'd live the rest of my life alone.

Dramatic, I know. If I had been conscious of it at the time, I would have rationally decided not to spiral and assured myself that I wasn't losing everyone. But emotions often don't play rationally. They show up in a blaze of glory, asking for something.

I was tangled up in knots by a fear I hadn't fully acknowledged and didn't totally understand.

The question was, what was I supposed to do with this feeling?

2

ALL TANGLED UP

I should mention that the mere fact that I was aware that Kate's dream of adventure was causing uncomfortable emotions and that I paused to process why was a bit of a breakthrough for me.

If you've read any of my previous books, you're probably accustomed to the fix-it vibe that flows through much of my writing. I'm a fixer at heart. I *love* to solve problems, whether for myself or others. I enjoy asking a thousand questions to get to the bottom of what's really going on with someone and then lay out a useful, hopefully not-scary, Bible-inspired solution for helping them get unstuck. Seriously, if life is like school, this process is like recess to me every time.

Helping people fix their problems has been a key motivation behind many of my previous books and is also why I founded IF:Gathering, a nonprofit organization committed to helping people growing in their faith and freedom.

For much of my adult life, I've loved this aspect of my personality, of my approach. I thought it was amazing. I mean, I think you'd agree that life is full of problems. Who doesn't have problems? And if problems abound for us all, then what's better than to have a helpful fixer around?

I considered my fix-it nature a gift—a spiritual gift, in fact. But over the past few years, as I've been on this journey toward untangling my emotions, I've come to see things in a very different light.

The truth is that I've been so busy fixing stuff that I've neglected the feeling part of me. Like I said earlier, every time I experienced sadness, fear, anger—any undesirable emotion, really—my brain would immediately click into fight mode, determined to fend off the feeling. I would line up my thoughts to attack the feeling and then condemn it, explaining to myself why I shouldn't feel it at all.

I was swift, and I was efficient.

Who needed feelings, anyway?

I haven't given myself permission to feel what I actually feel. I haven't given the people in my life permission to feel what *they* actually feel. It turns out you can't feel feelings while you're preoccupied with fixing them.

Recognizing this truth about myself has raised some questions for me. Like, why am I so quick to fix situations and adjust circumstances and alter my general reactions to life instead of feeling the feelings these dynamics bring up? Why do I consistently leapfrog over assessment straight into activity? Why am I seemingly allergic to introspection? What am I afraid of finding there?

Can you relate?

If I may be a bit presumptuous, I'll whisper this to you now: "You can relate—I know it. I'm certain you tend to resist examining *your* feelings too."

Part of being human is being tempted to solve problems rather than sit with them—it's what kept us alive in eras past. If a wild boar is on your tail, you'd better start running, right? No time to contemplate what happens in your heart and mind as fear rises in your chest. So we learned to run. We learned to flee, and we kept running. No time to sort out how we *feel* about things, lest that boar close the gap and mow us down.

Like I said, I deeply valued this fix-it approach, which I saw as something helpful about myself.

But over the past few years, as I've been learning to listen to what my emotions are trying to tell me, I've discovered a truth that shifted everything for me: **Feelings were never meant to be fixed; feelings are meant to be felt.**

For so long—too long, honestly—I didn't grasp this. I didn't like what emotions did to me. They were the reason my stomach felt sick when I was nervous or scared. They were the reason my chest tightened when I was reminded that the future was beyond my control. They were the reason tears would spring to my eyes whenever one of my kids took a harsh tone with me. And if they were to blame for so much discomfort and pain, why would I give them license to come in and just do as they pleased?

My feelings were trying to tell me something important, but I thought they were attempting to take over. And I wasn't about to let them take control.

Your feelings aren't trying to control you—they are trying to tell you something.

My fix-it approach kept me safe, or so I believed. This approach allowed me to run from my feelings and help those I love run from their feelings too. And for quite some time, this strategy worked. I learned to deflect with the best of them. I learned to deny how I truly felt.

When someone at work said something that hurt me, I would pretend I was fine and yet dwell on it every night as I was falling asleep.

When my kids came home from a hard day at school, I would try to get them to remember the good things that happened instead of sitting with them in the pain of hurts.

When I felt angry at my husband, I would pretend it was all okay and get on with my day, only to lose my temper a few weeks later over a list of stored-up offenses.

Even when I would have a dream day with my people all around me, if any happiness or joy sprang up, I felt a tinge of guilt because other things were getting ignored that needed my attention.

I was always telling myself why I shouldn't feel some way, and then I'd push it all down and go back to my day.

The downside? Nobody knew what was actually going on with me.

Nobody—including myself.

WE CAN'T GO ON LIKE THIS

A couple of years ago, I fell into an emotional pit that I wasn't sure how to emerge from. That season was actually the catalyst for my writing this book. Like so many people, I came out on the other side of the pandemic unsure how to thrive in a world that was so chaotic and unpredictable. One evening, I looked at Zac and said, "I can't do this anymore. Something is wrong. Really wrong. And while I don't have words to explain it, I can't go on this way."

I was numb.

Work and kids and life were demanding, and surviving a pandemic with its insecurities and unknowns had left us all a little wrung out. I was tired, but . . .

I wasn't mad.

I wasn't sad.

I wasn't enraged.

I wasn't annoyed.

I wasn't happy.

I didn't feel *anything*. That's what was wrong.

I remember sitting in a chair most mornings, alone with my Bible opened on my lap. I love reading my Bible. I've *always* loved God's Word. But as I'd sit there hoping for inspiration, my heart felt distant and cold. I knew something wasn't right and that I needed to figure it out, but the tangle felt impossible to undo. My stomach would turn. My chest would get tight. My shoulders would hunch forward. And often, I'd audibly sigh. These were all signs of emotions undealt with, but I didn't know that. Also, what I didn't realize then, but I'm starting to grasp now, is that I was in the best possible position, which was there in the presence of God, where the only feeling I seemed capable of was the simple *desire* to heal and grow.

IF COLLECTIVELY WE were stressed out *before* the pandemic, then we're way past meltdown status now. Either we've resigned ourselves to living numb—"How am I? Fine! Really, I'm good, so good! I'm good! I'm fine! And you?"—or we have handed over the steering wheel of our lives to our wild feelings and keep crashing into things as a result. I get it! Truly, I do.

Maybe you, like me, shut down anytime a feeling starts to head your direction. But perhaps you are on the other end of the spectrum, feeling so many feelings every minute that you can't imagine how on earth you are supposed to make sense of them. We all feel differently. And I want to say that wherever you fall on that spectrum, it makes sense. And we aren't all that different. We have feelings, and we are trying to figure out what to do with them.

Two years ago, when I felt like my heart had shut down, I decided that I'd give anything to *feel* again, to experience emotions once more. I didn't want to just survive. I wanted to feel. I wanted to be elated after having a dynamic conversation with friends I adore. I wanted to tear up upon hearing the beginning beats of "How Great Thou Art" in church. I wanted to feel even the emotions of frustration and grief if it meant feeling human again.

Numbness serves a purpose for a season—it does. Like the temporary shock I experienced when Zac was first hospitalized, it protects us from feeling everything that's hard all at once. It keeps us afloat when a tsunami of emotion gathers in our lives. It buys us a little time when we probably shouldn't be making big decisions, when the best thing we can do is wait.

Which is most likely why so many of us dealt with emotional numbness coming out of the Covid-19 pandemic. How were we supposed to process all that had unfolded in early 2020 without totally losing our minds? So much confusion. So much fear. So much death. It was a lot. Going numb was our collective safety net, the thing that kept us from all simultaneously hitting the ground.

Like I say, such numbness was a *gift*. For a time, anyway. Until it became the thing keeping us closed off from ourselves and our emotions even after the world reopened.

Years ago, I came across the eighteenth-century revivalist preacher Jonathan Edwards's personal resolutions for his life. In the same way that you or I might make a New Year's resolution that drives our behavior for that year—or at least until February, if we're like most people—Edwards wrote lifelong resolutions, which he reviewed once weekly, that reminded him of who he wanted to be, of the existence he wanted to pursue. There were seventy of these resolutions, and number six was this: "*Resolved, To live with all my might, while I do live.*"[1]

It seems like such an obvious objective, doesn't it—living while we live? But you've probably noticed that it's really, really difficult to live with all your might when you're settling for apathetic and numb.

Apathetic and numb aren't living at all.

Stay in that space very long and you'll miss your life. And nobody wants to do that.

To live is to feel, and to feel is to live.

Think about it: Have you ever had the experience of a family member telling a story about something that happened when you were two or three years old and, try as you might, you just can't remember that event? You were alive. You were present. The situation was impactful to other people who were there. But you have no recollection of what happened or why it mattered. Why? Because that memory isn't attached to any emotion for you. Emotion is how we experience life. Emotion is how we remember what happened.

Brain scans show that emotions directly trigger a response in the part of the brain called the amygdala. "The amygdala boosts memory encoding by enhancing attention and perception," say researchers from the Queensland Brain Institute, "and can help memory retention by triggering the release of stress hormones, such as adrenaline and cortisol, to boost arousal."[2] In other words, emotion is what makes events count.

If I asked you to describe a time during your childhood when you felt sad or mad or ridiculously happy or left out or admired or disappointed or afraid or extra-confident, my guess is that you could come up with a detailed story.

You would start telling me about crashing on your roller skates and ripping up your knee, or about whirling on the merry-go-round at your neighborhood playground as you stared at the clouds whirling by above, or about overhearing your parents arguing in the next room about what day Uncle Gene said he's coming to visit, or about the first time you got highlights and how that new look made you feel the next day at school.

Lead with emotion, and the memories *flow.*

That is why it's so damaging to kids to ignore, minimize, or reject altogether their feelings. To feel is to live, and to live is to feel. In his book *Emotionally Healthy Spirituality,* pastor and author Peter Scazzero wrote, "When we deny our pain, losses, and feelings year after year, we become less and less human. We transform slowly into empty shells with smiley faces painted on them."[3]

Without feelings, there is no life.

I'm writing this book not only to help us feel again but also to help us start living again.

With all our might, to *live.*

A VISION OF EMOTIONAL HEALTH

A couple of years ago, I wrote a book titled *Get Out of Your Head,* in which I explored at length the power you and I have to take control of our thoughts. I remember being lit up with the simplicity of cognition—the physiology and psychology and theology of how we think. It was a head book, full of practical tools so that whenever a negative thought tries to spin us out, we can remember the God-given power to choose to interrupt it and replace it. It was a book about agency. About intentionality. About *hope.* The realization that we can exercise power over our thoughts rather than living at their mercy brought new freedom to countless people, including me. I stand by every sentence I wrote. It's a great complement to everything we will discuss here.

But here's what's also true: I recognized even as I wrote that book that something lives underneath our thoughts. Thoughts don't manifest themselves out of nowhere; thoughts are driven by how we *feel.* Delving into that idea was beyond the scope of *Get Out of Your Head,* but it's truly the next logical step for anyone who wants to be free, whole, healthy, and connected to their people and God.

My recommendation to you as you read these chapters is to let both your head and your heart come to play. Let *all* of you have a seat at the table so that *all* of you can learn how to live fully, wholly, abundantly again—or maybe for the very first time.

When I first conceived of this book, an image came to mind. It was of a continuous, unbroken rope held in a triangular shape, anchored by figures standing at each of the three points: God, the people in our lives who love us, and us.

The rope was mostly smooth from point to point, clean and essentially unencumbered.

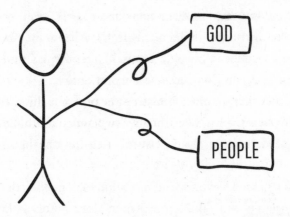

That rope represented our feelings and the way they are meant to work. As we'll explore in the pages to come, our emotions serve to connect us to God, to others, and to ourselves. But that image contrasts starkly with how most of us would describe our emotional inner lives: a jumble of confusion that has us tangled up in knots.

See, here is how it feels in reality:

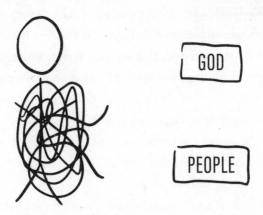

We want to connect our feelings to God to get them worked out, and we try to connect deeply with people, but it all feels like a mess.

Let me just say, I'm not a huge fan of knots. Yeah, knots help me keep my running shoes on my feet. I've heard they are helpful for Eagle Scouts and people who sail. And the few times I have rock climbed, they've made me feel much safer.

But most of the time, knots aren't helpful. Usually, they're hindrances to my goals, like when we've planned a fun family evening of decorating the Christmas tree but the lights are all tangled up.

Did you know—you are going to think I'm making this up, but I promise I'm not—that there is an entire field of mathematical study devoted to the study of knots? It's called, well, "knot theory."[4] And for the past couple hundred years, smart people who can't get enough of knots have sat around thinking about knots, deliberating how to quantify the number of crosses a given knot possesses, determining whether two differently shaped knots with the exact same number of crosses are in fact equivalent knots, and more.

Smart people figured out that by simply studying a knot—its size, its shape, its various crossings and parts—they could identify certain characteristics that would ensure a few simple moves could be used to undo that knot. And guess how they studied the knot?

By holding it up to the light.

The light in this metaphor is Jesus; it's the Word of God; it's ultimate truth. And the knots we need to untangle are the emotions we haven't yet brought to Him.

Over the past three years, I've committed myself to holding my tangled feelings to the light. And with each loosening of a knot, I've experienced more freedom—freedom to breathe, to laugh, to cry, to rage, to rejoice.

Freedom to live.

I've discovered a style of living in which other people could know me and (miracle!) I could also know them.

I could know myself—what I thought *and* what I felt.

I could know God.

I could live authentically connected to God.

I could learn to feel my feelings instead of pressuring myself to fix everything. (Spoiler: Very little ever *actually* got fixed.)

I could heal from a past marked by running.

I could experience real life, give myself permission to respond with real emotion, and even learn to enjoy it.

I could start to untangle the mess created when we refuse to take the time to work out the kinks in our connections between our loved ones and God and ourselves.

After decades spent skimming the surface, I could choose to finally go deep.

I could explore the emotional depth of life.

I could change.

I saw that there was another way to live—that by experiencing my feelings instead of stuffing them or denying them, I could live a far more fulfilling life. I learned that by sharing what I was feeling with real, live human beings, I could have deeper community than I'd ever experienced before. I learned that things could really change for me, that I could feel and heal and connect. I could help my brain form entirely different pathways. I could get all the kinks worked out of my rope. And I want to tell you, if you're struggling like I was, the same is true for you. Just like neurons that because of neuroplasticity literally reach out for each other to try to connect, you can reach for—and find every time—new pathways for living whole.

I am different now. Pathways have formed where they were severed. Authentic deep friendships exist where there was isolation. Emotional connection thrives where there was emotional aversion and unhealth.

I am whole and connected to my own heart and to other people. I've learned the ways and language of feeling. I've learned to unknot my tangled soul and allow God to pull me in to the deeper, fuller life He built for me.

I am different.

Please say you'll come with me for the chapters that follow. We need this.

At this point you might be thinking that the world has swung so far that emotions are everything. That's not what I'm saying, so please let me take a minute to put you at ease. We're talking about emotion that is submitted to the will of God and the truth of God's word. We're not talking about just feeling things and acting on them. We're talking about using them for the purposes God intended—for our emotions to connect us to each other and to God. But one reason that our feelings are coming out sideways everywhere is that we never learned how to do this right. So when we start healing, we begin to experience emotions how they're meant to be experienced. Then what happens? We start to regulate. It's a great word. It's a counseling word, but it's a spiritual word. It's what happens to our bodies. God built our nervous system.

I know we are all coming at this topic from different places. But hear me loud and clear: Whether you are a man or woman, young or old, big feeler of wild feelings or someone who just doesn't want to feel, an impassive man in his sixties who swears he has never cried or a preteen girl who can't seem to ever quit crying, **we are all feelers.**

We may express it in a million different ways or try to hold it in with a few techniques, but we all feel. God built us to feel.

There is a continuum:

People who never express their feelings	People who express all their feelings

Where do you fall on this spectrum?

Wherever you see yourself, I want you to know that as I've worked on this book, I've thought about both those of you who have a hard time expressing your feelings and those of you who feel as if you have so many wild emotions going every minute that you might explode.

This vision, this process, works for people on both ends of the spectrum and everyone in between. If you are someone who doesn't feel, I'm going to teach you how. Strike that. *God* is going to help you feel again in a healthy way, because that is what He wants. But if you feel like you're overrun with emotion, I'm going to help you slow down and take each feeling apart and notice it and name it and know what to do with it. Again, *God* will do the work through this process. It feels ironic to apply order and a process to something as mysterious and organic as emotions. But God is a God of order, and I am someone who appreciates order.

Let me remind you how valuable our feelings are. Let me prove to you how necessary they are to your vitality in relationships with others and to a sense of sustained connection with God. Let me lead you to a healthier way to experience all these feelings. Let me show you the moves—the twists, the passes, the neat limbo you can do under that pesky piece of emotional string—that will take you from emotionally stuck to emotional health, from apathetic to able to articulate what you feel, from distanced to connected to your own soul and others, and to a deeper and more robust connection with God. These are the by-products of an emotionally healthy person.

Emotional health is possible. It is possible to untangle the knots that may have built up over decades in your life. I know it seems impossible. It's not. I've seen it happen for me and so many people I love.

I'm going to show you how.

PART TWO

why we're so tangled up

3

WHERE DID
THE MESS BEGIN?

Feelings were never meant to be fixed; feelings are meant to be felt.

When you first read that assertion, what was your reaction? I would guess that, like the hundreds of people I've talked with—both online and one-on-one—as I've been writing this book, you had a visceral reaction to it. Why? For the straightforward reason that most of us from our earliest days were taught to not feel what we feel.

Regardless of the year you were born, the city you grew up in, and the specifics involving who raised you, I am confident you were conditioned right from the start regarding what to do when you felt a feeling.

Long before you and I could walk or talk or hold a spoon for ourselves, we were taught what to do when we felt happy, when we felt sad, when we felt angry, and when we felt agonizingly alone. We were taught how to deal—or not deal—with our emotions way back then. And we were model students who learned those lessons by heart, like immutable stories written deep into the crevices of our souls.

Somewhere from someone, most of us picked up the messages that we didn't *need* to feel sad, that we shouldn't be angry, and that it was illogical for us to feel scared. We learned to tell ourselves that we were okay or that the situation was okay or that the nebulous everything would be okay. We took note of the warnings that instead of sharing how we felt, the right thing for us to do was calm down or quit crying or spend a little time alone until we could pull ourselves together somehow.

We learned that strong emotions are uncomfortable and we shouldn't inflict them on others. We should smooth down their rough edges or, better yet, make them disappear.

These and other equally confusing messages were conveyed to us, and we believed them; we swallowed them whole. And so began our lifelong practice of denying ourselves permission to feel what we felt. Denying ourselves the truth of our humanity as beings created in the image of God—the God who feels all these feelings and created us to feel them as well.

WE ARE EMOTIONAL BEINGS

When I first looked into the eyes of my oldest son, Conner, I realized that he was already looking for me. He was the tiniest thing, just seven pounds, four ounces, a tiny ball of flesh and guts.

It would be months before he could form, let alone communicate, cohesive thoughts about life and the people he saw in the world. But there he was, scanning the horizon for me. He wanted his mama—that much he knew. He preferred me. He sensed cold water and hunger pangs . . . and me. When he cried and I would wrap him up in a warm blanket and hold him and issue shushing noises as I vigorously rocked him, he was comforted. He was safe and soothed and seen.[1]

And it helped.

Every bit of it helped.

Now, you tell me: How did my little seven-pound human know that he was unhappy or longing for comfort or that he wanted me? I'll tell you how: He *felt*. He felt all those feelings in his body and heart before he could ever form linear, clear thoughts, and to this day, he's still faithful to feeling. He still feels discomfort and longing and ten million other emotions, both fleeting and lasting—emotions that have shaped the man he is.

We come into the world not primarily as people who think but as people who feel.

Emotions flood through our bodies and souls—our mind, will, and emotions—reminding us of this truth. They don't stop at assigned places, and when we try to stem their flow, we fail. They course through us as they will, connecting the various parts of us to one another—connecting us to ourselves, connecting us to other people, connecting us to God. Feelings are the flowing river that connects the world in despair when an earthquake steals thousands of lives or in universal belly laughter at the perfect, brilliant Super Bowl commercial.

Connection.

Emotion connects us.

Our willingness to feel what we feel connects us to ourselves, to others, and to God.

So, how did we become tangled up, utterly unsure of how we should feel about our feelings?

THE MESSAGES WE PASS ALONG

Somewhere along the way, we've heard messages that teach us not to feel. Maybe from a parent who resents a child's feelings or feels judged by them. *We take great care of your every need. What possible reason do you have to feel rejected/sad/mad?*

Sometimes parents want to control our emotions to avoid embarrassment. *Do you have to make a scene in public?*

Sometimes they ignore our feelings so they don't have to acknowledge their own.

And so they often accidentally shame us for feeling things. They dismiss the feelings we felt. They neglect or ignore altogether the emotions we are juggling. They shut down as we try to engage.

"Knowing your true emotions and thoughts probably felt dangerous if it threatened to distance you from the people you depended on," wrote author Lindsay Gibson in her book *Adult Children of Emotionally Immature Parents.* "You learned that your goodness or badness lay not only in your behavior, but in your mind as well. In this way, you may have learned the absurd idea that you can be a bad person for having certain thoughts and feelings, and you may still hold that belief."[2]

As I'm laying this out, I so wish I could talk to you in person: What is *your* story here? Were you ever told by a parent or family member not to feel something that you really and truly felt? Were you ever told to calm down because your natural reaction was too big?

Of course, our parents were just passing along the same messages they'd learned as children. They probably learned how to not feel feelings from *their* parents, who probably got those messages from theirs.

But the consequences add up, generation after generation, unless we find a way to break the cycle.

ZAC AND I both grew up in families that loved us and were godly, but like many families, emotions weren't really talked about much. My husband comes from a football family; his dad is a coach and he was the quarterback. Emotions were something that could get in the way of the job he had to do. So he kept his head down, set a good example, and figured out how to suppress any negative emotion so that he could be effective at his sport. Even after wins, he learned not to celebrate for long because there was another game coming fast. His steely unemotional focus was an asset on the field.

Similarly, I grew up with a steadfast midwestern mother and a father who was raised in a military family. In short: I learned to think instead of feel. It's not so much that my parents shamed me for feeling; it's just that feelings weren't exactly flying around.

I don't remember feeling sad.

I don't remember feeling angry.

I don't remember feeling tons of happiness, though I'm certain I did.

Through elementary school. Through junior high. Through high school. Think, think, think; don't feel. Then came my college years, and suddenly my heart woke up. Everything was new and a little scary, and boy, did I start to feel. I felt sad. I felt lonely. I felt angry. I felt thrilled. I felt every feeling, all at once. And I loved it.

Throughout those first few months as a freshman at the University of Arkansas, I felt . . .

- deeply moved whenever I'd worship

- the most profound adoration for a senior boy who wouldn't give me the time of day

- frustrated that friends kept borrowing my clothes and forgetting to give them back

- perpetually worried about measuring up and meeting the constant demands of my brand-new life

By the time stoic Zac married me, I had *all* the feelings and wasn't afraid to express them. It was overwhelming for him. Like clockwork, we had arguments week after week that centered on my need for him to show up emotionally in our marriage and his refusal/inability to do so.

I should mention here that I have been married to Zac Allen for more than twenty-five years and am madly in love with him. Also true: Our early days were a little . . . rough. We didn't really fight—it wasn't like that. It was more of a cold, cold war. I missed the people I'd emoted with, the friends I'd recently moved away from. But here's the thing: I'd been a model citizen in thinking land before. I knew how to thrive in this place.

We did our jobs. We went to Walmart. We ate dinner. We went to Fuddruckers for cheap cheeseburgers on weekend date nights.

As weeks eased into months and months turned into years, I thought about how much easier life was now that I didn't have to feel. It was more efficient. More sanitary. Less dramatic. Less mysterious.

Less . . . fun.

We were growing more and more distant, and I noticed myself talking more to my friends about things that were happening in my life than to Zac. We were simply roommates.

Wanting to go deeper, wanting more for our relationship but not knowing what we needed, I made an appointment with a marriage counselor. Zac reluctantly agreed to attend, and over the next few months, my unfeeling, stone-faced husband became flooded with every emotion imaginable. He learned to feel his feelings, and over the course of a year and a half, my emotionally absent husband became the emotional equivalent of Niagara Falls: lots of impressive presence, lots and *lots* of tears. But there was also a deeper connection with Jesus . . . and with me. *My* feelings woke up and felt safe again too. We were finally able to argue. We connected at a deeper level than I thought possible. And except for the fact that it took almost two years of counseling and hard work, the result was . . . magical. It really was.

Zac and I have enjoyed a whole string of emotionally attached years that I look back on with gratitude and joy. If there is any reason that our marriage has survived so many rough patches, it is that, by God's grace, we are building on the strong foundation we started with those emotionally healthy years.

THE CONFLICTING MESSAGES OF CHURCH AND CULTURE

I'll tell you more about my husband's emotional journey in coming pages, but right now I just want to let you know that things really can change. We don't have to stay where we are.

But **we can't experience emotional health on autopilot.** And the voices sending us confusing messages are so very loud.

Our families aren't the only ones passing along harmful messages about our feelings.

Many followers of Jesus have shared with me how much hurt and confusion has come into their lives because the church has denied their emotional realities, saying things like:

Emotions are dangerous.

Emotions are not reliable.

You should just push that feeling away.

Don't let your feelings control you.

Don't trust your feelings; just trust God.

In my own life, it was not uncommon for the sermon on Sunday to reference the words of the Old Testament prophet Jeremiah, who said that the human heart "is deceitful above all things, and desperately sick," concluding with the rhetorical question "Who can understand it?"[3] Absolutely, we shouldn't trust our feelings then, as they were destined to mislead us.

I went along with this logic. Who wants to be misled?

And the logic played out when I looked around at our generation, obsessed with our feelings.

Because following our feelings into destruction is certainly a familiar practice. Feelings minus God's wisdom can absolutely lead to a selfish life, all in the name of "Follow your heart! Your feelings are the only things that matter." That alternative message was not right either.

The world has gone full steam ahead to give all its energy to being led by our feelings.

If you don't feel in love, leave your spouse.

If you feel unhappy, sacrifice anything and everything to find happiness.

If you don't feel respected by your friends, ditch them and find new friends.

If God doesn't feel real to you, He probably isn't.

If any number of selfish behaviors feel right to you, it really doesn't matter how those things affect you or others. If it feels right, do it.

Feelings are everything! Follow your heart!

Let me be clear, you will never be emotionally healthy outside the will of God.

Just like your emotions were designed by God, the patterns and ways we are to live and thrive were also designed by God. You were built for obedience to a loving Father. The Fall disrupted that, but life is found inside His ways and will. And we know the will of God for our lives because of the gift of the Bible.

Therefore, "Ignore your feelings and just pursue Christ" sounds exactly right in comparison to the world's shout of "Obey your feelings," especially given where emotions running wild can lead us. So ignore your emotions. Control them. That's what all "good Christians" do, because feelings are the enemy, right?

Except for one huge problem. Actually, two:

1. Denying our feelings isn't working. Divorces, abuse, and mental-health issues are all over the church. We aren't experiencing a healthier, more abundant life, mainly because we are ignoring our feelings and treating them like the enemy.

2. God feels! He feels big feelings, as we will see from Genesis to Revelation, and He made us to feel, created it all inside us. So, emotions can't be evil. They must be good gifts if God feels them and built them for us.

Denying and ignoring our feelings are just not viable options.

In defense of the contemporary church, I should mention here that this outright denial of human emotion I learned in seminary goes back hundreds, if not thousands, of years.[4]

In the early years of the church, emotions were viewed with suspicion. They were associated with the sinful nature of humanity. Asceticism encouraged the suppression and denial of emotions, punishing the body as evil and using "rigorous self-discipline, severe abstinence, austerity" to try to beat the body into submission.[5]

Since the body was not spiritual, the thinking went, the body should be considered evil and wholly denied, even punished if it feels something wrong. So, the super-religious were skeptical of anything the body was telling them. Ignore the body and focus solely on God. Yet the body is one of the main ways we notice and engage our emotions. Our physical bodies are designed by God and are gifts from Him to care for and notice and steward here.

During the Middle Ages, the expression of intense emotions was encouraged in private devotional practices. This isn't to say you'd go telling your people how you felt, though. In those days, proper Christians kept much of that to themselves.

Throughout the Renaissance and Enlightenment periods, emotions were seen as irrational and unreliable. This belief led to a decline in the importance placed on emotions in religious practice, and a focus on intellectual pursuits prevailed.

A generation of baby boomers who often prized reason and rational thinking and rarely shared their emotions ironically raised a younger generation that swung far to the other side: Emotions are everything. When I was refreshing all my church history with my favorite seminary professor, he said something else that deserves a mention. He said that in recent generations, "emotions in the church are seen as feminine. Christian stereo-types developed as the 'emotional woman' and the 'stoic, non-emotional male' as the standard and as the goal."

The church has spent a lot of time in confusion about how we are all supposed to feel.

A BETTER WAY

What if emotions in and of themselves are not the problem here? What do we do with them if our feelings are divinely built into us, on purpose and for a purpose? I happen to believe that's true, and here in a few pages, I will work to persuade you to see it too.

I can confidently tell you that this is not a book about being controlled by our emotions. Emotions cannot and must not rule our days, our lives. But equally, this is *not* a book about our controlling our emotions.

I believe there's a third way—an emotionally secure, connected, life-giving way that God has for us that could set us free to love and connect and live more deeply than we knew was possible.

Because feelings aren't meant to be fixed. Feelings are meant to be felt.

4

THE TRUTH ABOUT
YOUR FEELINGS

In digging into the science of emotions over these past few years, I've become convinced that emotions are not meant to control us; they are meant to *inform* us. To alert us. To connect us. To remind us that we're alive and to help us make sense of the world around us.

Did you know that the mental structures that process emotions are located deeper in the brain than where the thinking structures live?[1]

Did you know that what you believe about the world in which you live, even if those beliefs reside on a subconscious level, can cause stress in the body that leads to actual disease?[2]

Did you know that when you cry, your tears literally detoxify your body, raising oxytocin and activating your nervous system so that your body can find calm again?[3] Or that when you exercise regularly, you experience anxiety less often?[4]

All of this and more is governed by our feelings. Feelings that come to us in three distinct ways:

1. Feelings show up in our minds.

2. Feelings show up in our bodies.

3. Feelings show up in our actions.

You've probably noticed that whenever something happens that makes you feel something, you feel it in more ways than one. For example, certain memories are triggered whenever you experience a particular emotion.

In that situation I described earlier regarding Kate's maybe move, I was only eighteen months removed from Zac's near-death experience. But it was all right there in my mind, in my body, in *me*.

Just after Zac came home from the hospital, our entire family took CPR classes so that if anything happened, we would know what to do. Let me just tell you that watching one's kids learn to resuscitate a dummy that is meant to represent your husband while said hubby is upstairs, incapable of getting out of bed, is something I still cry thinking about.

During Zac's more lucid moments, we spent our time discussing delightful subjects such as wills and end-of-life instructions and the to-do list I'd need to address should the unthinkable unfold.

All this was traumatic enough on its own, but the fear of losing Zac and Kate and being left alone was likely tangled up with an earlier emotional memory that I'd never fully grappled with.

I was seven years old when my great-grandmother Munsy died. I didn't know her well, but whenever my parents made an obligatory visit, I went along to her house in my smocked dress, with barrettes in my hair. A cuckoo clock hung on her wall, and every single hour, the bird would come out and squeal to alert us another hour had passed. Now I can't imagine having that clock in my life, but man, I thought it was cool back then.

That's about all I knew of Munsy. I never met her husband or caught even a glimmer of her personality. To me, she seemed old and tired and boring except for her cuckoo clock. But after her funeral, as we drove the hour back to Little Rock, I cried. I remember distinctly not wanting my parents to know I was crying. I think I felt guilty for being sad. I don't remember them crying, so why should I cry over someone I barely knew? I was looking out the window at the stars. What made me cry wasn't sadness over the loss of Munsy, even though I tried to muster that up. What made me cry was the thought of death, the unknown, and the realization that no one could protect me from it, not even my parents, if it came for me. I knew at the age of seven that I would have to die alone and no one could die with me. *Seven!*

Though I didn't make the connection in my thoughts, that gaping abyss of aloneness made its presence known through my tumultuous emotions each time I thought of losing my dear ones.

I'm confident you could identify a similar situation of seemingly random feelings that are rooted in your past. When big, perhaps seemingly illogical emotions come up in response to something, you feel it in your lived experience—have you felt this way before? What happened back then? Where did things lead?

You feel it in your physical body—racing heart, tensed-up shoulders, upset stomach, and the like.

And you feel it in your reaction—"I now feel *happy* [or *sad, regretful, excited, afraid*]." And that probably comes out some way in words or actions, perhaps for good or maybe a little sideways or even flat-out wrong.

NAVIGATING THE RIVER OF EMOTION

I canoe. I mean, I own a canoe. Actually two. We have some land in the middle of hot Texas, and there's not much to do out there except canoe.

I'm the worst canoer you've ever met. Well, I think I'm good. I paddle with great confidence. I boss the other people paddling along with me in my canoe. But bottom line: The boat never goes where I want it to. We hit the shore and zigzag around the river. Everyone with us can't figure out why. *I* can't figure out why, and I've been doing this awhile! I know the goal is to stay in the middle of the river, so we're burning a lot of energy weaving across.

Psych 101 would tell you that emotional regulation is the goal. I want you to picture that river and my canoe. On one side of the river is explosion, anger, weeping, gnashing of teeth, deep-seated feelings, throwing dishes, beating someone up. I know we've talked a lot about the gift of emotions, but we all know what happens when we let them run the show. On the other side of the river is shutting down, not feeling anything, dismissing all you feel, and imagining you don't feel. These are the two banks we want to avoid hitting in our emotional canoe.

Now, what's interesting is that trauma causes your river to start rushing even faster and brings the banks way too close. Of course you're going to hit them. You've been through the death of a loved one or abuse or even a move or job loss, something that has caused your river to narrow way down. Your capacity to deal with the emotions you will inevitably encounter on a day-to-day basis has just shrunk.

And that's okay!

If you're reading this and you have been through something difficult and feel easily irritated, maybe swinging into deep, unhealthy emotion or even checking out, I'm gonna say what I always say:

Of course you are. You're fragile. You're not yourself. All our rivers at different points in our life shrink and get narrow. Each time is an opportunity to come back to Jesus, over and over again.

If you're in this season right now, ask the people around you for grace. And don't be afraid to get help.

But if you're in a wide part of the river and feel emotionally stable and healthy, I urge you not to get complacent or look down on those who are struggling. Difficult circumstances may be around the bend for you. Enjoy this season. Feel the feelings. Share your guts about the small- or medium-sized things going on in your life. But don't judge the people who haven't quite reached the wider, calmer section of their river.

One of my kids has been through so much trauma they could write their own book. And what others might mistakenly view as a behavior problem is so clearly just a place where they need some extra grace to process their big emotions, which are intensified by life's past hits. They need a little more time to figure out how to navigate the rocks of life and avoid slamming into the riverbank. And as we have given that kid grace, they have begun to process in a healthier way and their river widens.

Our rivers can widen. With safe places to process and sometimes professional help, our capacity to regulate our emotions grows.

IT'S NOT A BUG—IT'S A FEATURE

As we've seen, our feelings show up in our minds, bodies, and reactions. That's where we experience them. But where do they come from?

They were built into us by a God who feels. **We were designed by God to feel.**

I follow Jesus. And whether you follow Him too or have no faith at all or are still deciding what you believe, I'm glad you are here. If you don't know Him, I'm guessing that as you keep reading, you'll really like Him. Because as you will see, He is compassionate toward you, toward me. This matters because to be human is to long for compassion. We're all starving for compassion, and Jesus wants to provide it.

When Jesus walked the earth, story after story of His ministry confirmed how He cared about each person He came across. He cared about their mind. He cared about their body. He cared about their soul. He even cared about their emotions, which is something we don't hear too much about.

You know, I've heard smart Bible people teach and preach on how important it is for us to believe certain things with our minds and behave certain ways with our bodies and commit to certain things, but I can't think of a single time when I heard someone teach on how *Jesus* feels about the emotions *we* feel. Which is odd to me because all throughout Scripture, we see evidence of God the Father, God the Son, and God the Spirit feeling lots and lots of feelings.

How do you think God feels about your feelings? Is He judging them?

. . .

As I began my research on this, I had so many questions:

When does feeling an emotion turn sinful?

Have all the emotions always existed?

Will they exist forever in heaven?

What does God do with His emotions?

Wait, does God have emotions?

Does the Bible say we can control our emotions?

If we can, does that mean we should?

While I cannot answer these questions exhaustively, these pages are my attempt to explore what God's Word says.

At the very least, I had to know, *Are my feelings sin?*

It doesn't take long in Genesis to see that they cannot be sin, because God himself feels! He feels happiness about everything He created and disappointment at His creation's rebellion. He feels anger at their continued rebellion. He feels delight when Abraham and David and others follow Him and sadness when they go their own ways.

Time and again, we see God express His compassion toward humanity as He gives them just one more chance to obey His commands. And then one more chance after that. As the Bible says, "The Lord is not slow to fulfill his promise as some count slowness, but is patient toward you, not wishing that any should perish, but that all should reach repentance."[5] Because of His great love for His children, God reaches for a relationship with them. He does this through judges and through prophets and through priests.

I see you.

I love you.

Will you choose to love Me too?

It will take the ultimate sacrifice—His ultimate sacrifice—to win them back.

He knows this.

But still, He tries.

This radical love of God is exactly what Jesus came to earth to demonstrate. He came in the flesh to bear witness to the idea that God was looking for us already and hoped that we'd come looking for Him too.

The prophet Isaiah referred to Jesus as "a man of sorrows and acquainted with grief."[6] Before we see Jesus face the Cross in the Garden of Gethsemane, we get a glimpse into an intimate moment within the three persons of the Trinity, when Jesus is so troubled and afraid that He sweats drops of blood. Fully aware that He is absolutely about to die on a cross, He asks His Father for another way, a path out of this peril and pain.[7]

Ultimately, He chooses the way of His Father to save us. He does this because of love.

Oh yes, God feels all the emotions. God the Father and God the Son and God the Spirit.

God the Spirit—He's real feely. Each member of the Trinity is, but Scripture says we can grieve particularly the Spirit.[8] In the book of James, it says the Spirit is jealous for us when we want the things of the world.[9]

The Spirit can communicate our heart's cry to the Father when we have no words.[10]

If God is an unchangeable eternal being who feels, then we know that emotions were not created. Emotions have always been, and emotions will always be.

Because of this, emotions are simply another facet of what it means to be made in the image of God. Therefore, emotions are not bad, and emotions are not sin. Emotions aren't even neutral. When we understand that God has a purpose and plan for them, emotions are actually good—and not just some of them, like peace and joy, but all of them.

All emotions are good.

Aren't you just blown away by this? A God who feels all the feelings and does not sin, He appropriates all those feelings rightly. Just like with so many aspects of God, it's impossible to get our heads fully around a God who feels all the emotions but does not sin.

The author of Hebrews says of Jesus, "We have not an high priest which cannot be *touched with the feeling* of our infirmities; but was in all points tempted like as we are, *yet without sin.*"[11] In the coming pages, we'll look at several moments when Jesus felt His emotions and allowed them to draw people to Himself and didn't sin.

But for now, just let this sink in: **Emotions are not the sin; it's what we do with them that is the sin.**

Emotions have always been, and emotions always will be, though certainly in heaven our need for sadness and fear and anger will disappear, as Scripture promises.

OUR LINKS TO A RICHER, FULLER LIFE

The more I dug into the whole idea that emotions come from God, who is also a feeling being, the more frustrated I became that I was never taught about any of this. Finding shockingly little theological academic work on the subject, I phoned my favorite seminary professor, who happens to be one of the most brilliant people I know, and peppered him with questions. Several times he paused, unsure of how to respond. More than once, the words "I don't know" actually came out of his mouth. As he wondered aloud why there isn't more theological study on emotions, he said, "I guess the thinkers never stopped to think about feelings."

He's probably right. And it's really too bad, because feeling things is often precisely how we connect to God.

Think about it:

Joy often incites gratitude and worship.

Anger can be a tool wielded against injustices.

Regret is a reminder of our need for God's forgiveness.

Sadness makes us draw near to God for comfort.

Fear can provide protection to help us discern right paths.

Even hate and jealousy, which we see in God's own display of emotions, can be good. Like notes of music or shades of color, emotions bring texture and variety into our lives. They can reveal something about our humanity and the lives we are living.

At the same time, it's important to acknowledge that emotions, like many good things that God created—think *sex, money, power*—can lead us to sin. We know this. We see this dynamic at work everywhere we look.

So, when does an emotion become a sin? It's interesting that in the Bible, emotions aren't the sin. For example, "Be angry and do not sin."[12] The potential for sin seems to lie in our response to our anger.

Historically, in the Christian faith, the soul has been viewed as being made up of three parts: our thoughts, our emotions, and our will.

Jesus taught us that if we even think about sleeping with our neighbor's spouse, we have sinned,[13] so we know that we can sin in our thoughts. It is possible that, when you feel angry, you begin to feed your thoughts, to dwell in your mind hour after hour on your anger. As you feed it and feed it, that emotion that was not in itself a sin can give way to hateful thoughts of revenge and maybe even become a toxic stronghold. That was the great breakthrough many of us found in *Get Out of Your Head*—that God can rescue us from spirals of toxic thinking! We cannot forget the power we have over our thought lives and how intentionally choosing gratitude and service and connection can shift our minds and often bring healing in our emotional lives too.

A lot of that power to shift comes from a third part of our souls: the will. This is truly my favorite part of the way God built us. We are humans with power and choice. We are not controlled by God, as if we were robots. We also, if we have accepted the salvation Jesus offers, are not controlled by our desires and sin. The apostle Paul described it as our freedom to move toward God on paths of peace and life or to choose paths of sin and death and destruction.[14] We make these choices every day, dozens of times.

As we consider the relationship between sin and our feelings in the light of our souls, an image comes to mind, adapted from one my friend Cassie often uses in her work as a licensed counselor. Think of your soul as a train, with a single engine pulling two cars. If your emotions are the engine, they're going to take you off a cliff! But if your will, submitted to God, is powering your train, then your emotions and thoughts are free to follow, connected securely so everything travels together in beauty and freedom and safety.

We cannot help but feel emotions, and we should allow ourselves to feel them—but in a redeemed way, a life-giving way, a way that leads to connection and greater freedom. Our emotion is not sin, but through our choices we determine whether our will and thoughts either help or undermine our ability to live wholeheartedly. Feelings can lead to good, and they can lead to bad, even as they themselves are gifts from God.

But imagine if our relational God, who created us in love to be relational beings, had not given us all these emotions.

We'd never feel grateful.
So we'd never worship God.

We'd never feel mad.
So we'd never be propelled to take action against injustice.

We'd never feel love.
So we'd never fall in love or weep at the birth of a child.

We'd never be afraid.
So we'd never lean into someone for comfort or turn to God for help.

. . .

Take away emotions and we lose all the most intimate and sacred parts of life, the deepest parts of who we are. Would you be who you are without the moments of joy and the seasons of hard?

Think about three big moments in your life. Most of our memories we can recall because they were associated with strong emotion. When you think of those moments, what do you feel? What made each moment a core memory?

Now imagine if you didn't have any reaction to those moments, if you were numb, devoid of feeling.

Would anything mean anything at all?

Maybe life is so painful right now that numb actually sounds appealing to you. If so, I want you to know we have a God who issues descriptions of heaven as a place where He will personally, intimately wipe every tear from our eyes. A God who wants to pull you close today and hold you and be with you saying, "I have you. I love you." A God who not only feels for Himself but also comes close to us when we're feeling all *our* feelings too.

God is waiting for us to come to Him with all of it. Even the ugly feelings you and I are tempted to judge—God is waiting to see if we'll let them draw us back to Him.

5

EXPERTS IN
EVASIVE MEASURES

Whenever you feel an overwhelming feeling—sadness, say, or disappointment, anger, rejection, fear, or even joy or hope—you have a choice to make. Same goes for me. We can engage directly with that emotion and take it to God, or we can resist it, trying to evade what feels uncomfortable, embarrassing, maybe even painful. Often, we choose the latter option—mostly because we're afraid that if we engage directly, we'll crumble under the weight of our feelings.

Speaking for myself, I have a long history of opting out of sadness, anger, and fear. I often achieve this through a beautifully curated internal speech with a little spirituality thrown in for extra believability.

My brain preaches something like this:

Jennie, I know there is more stress around _____ [fill in the blank] than you can deal with, but if you focus on that you will crumble, and that will do no one any good. So, here is what is real: God loves you, you are fine, and everything is going to be okay. So get over it and do your day.

. . .

Convincing, right? You are probably thinking, *Why is this so bad? Trust God. Don't spin. Stuff it. Sounds good to me.*

Yes, you are right. It isn't all bad. In fact, in certain seasons it is all we can do to make it through the day. We can't crumble, so we turn to what I call the Three Cs:

Control. We try our hardest to take charge of our situation or other people in the hopes of making everything a little more desirable, a little more manageable.

Cope. We distract ourselves by turning to busyness or a favorite diversion for comfort.

Conceal. We stuff down that feeling and attempt to cover it up.

And sometimes we do all three at the same time.

Let's look a bit more closely at our three go-to responses. Although you likely turn to each of them in different circumstances, I'm betting one is your default mode. Getting honest with yourself here will free you to pursue the alternative we'll look at in the next chapter—a path of engagement that leads toward the emotional health your heart is longing for.

WE CONTROL

We have very understandable motivations for grasping at control. We want to feel good about ourselves, for starters. And when we sense that we're in control of a situation, our confidence can't help but go up.

We also seek control because it preserves our hope about the world in which we live. If you and I truly believe that we are in control of a situation—a birthday party, a relational mishap, a work meeting, a tense conversation, a child's misbehavior, and so forth—then we can hold on to the expectation that everything will turn out fine.

Without that sense of control?

Well, how do we cope with *that*?

So, we go at life with confidence and competence to spare.

We believe we can out-smart our adversaries, out-plan our catastrophes, and out-think every challenge we face. Sure, we pray. We ask others to pray for us. We exercise and get plenty of rest so that we're on our game. We eat steel-cut oatmeal because every time we eat steel-cut oatmeal, things go well for us. We mull previous situations, learning every lesson we can. We give ourselves little pep talks: "You can do this. You. Really. Can."

And sometimes we can. Sometimes the way out of sadness or a cranky mood really is to make our bed, take a shower, and conquer the day. Sometimes that is enough, and tomorrow things will look up. It's true.

But **if all we do is control or manage our emotions, we lose touch with ourselves, our need for God, and our need for each other.** Control shuts us down. Not just the difficult-to-face emotion we don't want to feel, but also our enjoyment of our friendships, the depth of prayer, the tears that used to pop up when we sang "Amazing Grace" at church, the creativity that used to inspire words or art or fun in our lives. It all gets shut out if we try to shut out some of it.

Attempting to control emotion requires so much effort. It's downright exhausting.

In fact, most of the time when we work to control an emotional outcome, we have no idea that's what we're doing. As far as we know, we're over here minding our own business, just busily living our lives. Many times, when we bump into an unfortunate set of events, our minds and bodies run a split-second assessment of our well-being, and as they determine the best course of action for keeping us comfortable and safe, they cast aside some emotions and allow others to bubble up.

I'll show you what I mean. Remember that situation with Kate possibly moving out of state or out of the country? Instead of my feeling sad or disappointed, which would have been a normal reaction to such dreaming, my heart began racing with anxiety, with a little "This isn't fair" in the back of my head. It would definitely feel terrifying to be abandoned. Far better to just feel stressed. And truthfully, I would never have dealt with the fear of abandonment except that I couldn't shake the thought that there had to be more to my reaction. And there was.

This is why, in part 3, I'm going to teach you how to sit with your emotions long enough to understand what they're really about. As I have already mentioned, there are always things beneath the things. And it is hauntingly true.

For now, I want to help you assess how deep your desire for emotional control runs.

Here's how this will work: After you read each statement, rate yourself on the accompanying scale. A rating of "1" means you never deal with the tendency in question. A rating of "2" means you rarely do. A rating of "3" means you often do. A rating of "4" means *Have you been reading my texts?*

1. **I pay attention to my body's physical cues during high-stress situations and conversations.**

   ☐ 1 (Never) ☐ 2 (Rarely) ☐ 3 (Often) ☐ 4 (Always)

2. I pay attention to my mind's thoughts during high-stress situations and conversations.

   ☐ 1 (Never)   ☐ 2 (Rarely)   ☐ 3 (Often)   ☐ 4 (Always)

3. I pay attention to my authentic feelings during high-stress situations and conversations.

   ☐ 1 (Never)   ☐ 2 (Rarely)   ☐ 3 (Often)   ☐ 4 (Always)

4. I trust myself to feel whatever it is I truly feel.

   ☐ 1 (Never)   ☐ 2 (Rarely)   ☐ 3 (Often)   ☐ 4 (Always)

5. I am unafraid to share with others how I feel.

   ☐ 1 (Never)   ☐ 2 (Rarely)   ☐ 3 (Often)   ☐ 4 (Always)

6. I am patient with myself regarding my emotional reality, even when it changes more frequently than I would prefer.

   ☐ 1 (Never)   ☐ 2 (Rarely)   ☐ 3 (Often)   ☐ 4 (Always)

7. I stay engaged with myself and others, even when things feel emotionally intense.

   ☐ 1 (Never)   ☐ 2 (Rarely)   ☐ 3 (Often)   ☐ 4 (Always)

8. I stay calm and centered, even when my emotional reality feels undesirable.

   ☐ 1 (Never)   ☐ 2 (Rarely)   ☐ 3 (Often)   ☐ 4 (Always)

9. I stay curious with myself regarding the emotional experiences that unfold.

   ☐ 1 (Never)   ☐ 2 (Rarely)   ☐ 3 (Often)   ☐ 4 (Always)

10. **I remain grateful for emotions as they surface for me, even when they are ones I might not have chosen.**

☐ 1 (Never) ☐ 2 (Rarely) ☐ 3 (Often) ☐ 4 (Always)

Here's the complicated thing about control: It earns praise from everyone. If you can control your emotions, you look healthy. You look unfazed when the boss is frustrated with you. You look confident when you've been left out of a fun gathering. You smile at your kid as they express deep despair because of a problem at school. You look perfectly in control and drama-free, a quality highly prized in the world around us. I get it! But come close and let me tell you . . .

That's jacked up.

I'm not saying we should instead yell at our kid or respond to our boss with anger. But we are feeling those feelings, and there is a time and place to be honest about them. And that begins by being honest with ourselves.

Controlling our emotions is not the goal. Healing them and expressing them in a healthy way is.

WE COPE

It's said of Winston Churchill that he often worked from his bed or his bathtub.

I get it.

He was emotionally carrying the weight of the world, sending thousands to their deaths during World War II, trying to win a war for the future of humankind. The guy deserved a few comforts while he tried to carry all that.

You probably get it too.

We run to any comfort we can find when we are in the thick of it, right?

In the world of psychology, a coping mechanism is anything we do to make it through an emotional beatdown. That's not the official scientific definition, but based on my lived experience, it's pretty accurate. And about 77 percent of us have turned to "addictive behaviors or unhealthy coping mechanisms" in response to mental-health challenges like depression and anxiety, according to Myriad Genetics nationwide survey.[1]

The list of coping mechanisms is nearly endless: procrastination, lethargy, drug use, indulging in unhealthy amounts of food or alcohol, oversleeping, self-harm, social isolation, workaholism, online shopping, obsessive-compulsive behaviors, and more.

Maybe you reach for new episodes to watch . . . busying hobbies . . . another drink—anything, really, to drown out how you feel.

Maybe the way you get around feeling your feelings is by scrolling social media for hours on end.

Maybe you phone a friend and blow your energy gossiping.

Maybe you work and work and work, thinking you'll find meaning if you finally succeed.

Maybe you shop and shop and shop online because it just plain makes you feel better.

Maybe you get lost in anything that helps you forget.

I've never done any of these things. Never. *Ha!*

Of course, some of our coping mechanisms are, on the surface, fairly innocuous and not altogether unhealthy. From time to time, our bodies need to decompress. My two personal favorite ways to cope are bingeing shows on Netflix and eating vast quantities of queso with my best friends.

As enjoyable as those things are, the relief they bring is momentary; the distraction and satisfaction is always short-lived, especially if we never deal with the things beneath the things. And I've noticed in my own life and in the lives of many people I know well that what begins as an every-once-in-a-while coping mechanism can become an everyday habit, and potentially an addiction, in very little time.

Whether or not we care to admit it, the reason we pursue avoidance through coping mechanisms is that we are unwilling to address—or incapable of doing so—our true emotional states. *We cannot deal with how we feel, so we go searching for an escape hatch instead.*

Then let me ask you: What are your favorite choices when it comes to coping?

We are making ourselves sick with our coping. We think that, in our checking out and numbing out, we are relaxing, but the truth is, we are missing the gifts of God that are meant to keep us in delightful relationship with Him. We are drifting from deep, meaningful relationships with other people in our coping.

In the pages to come, we're going to learn how to process our feelings effectively in real time. Before we do that, though, please open up your Bible and read Psalm 38. It offers such a powerful reminder of what its author, David, knew so well: There is a place to take our disappointment. There is a place to take our anger. There is a place to take our bitterness and frustration. There is a place to take our loneliness and boredom. We can take it all to Jesus. We can take it to Him and say, "Help me process this." "Help me be with You." "Help me to be still and not need to look at my phone." "Help me not to choose alcohol at night."

WE CONCEAL

When our oldest son, Conner, was two years old, soon after his baby sister arrived, I decided we needed an outing. So, we loaded up the car and went to the mall with my mom and sister. Somehow in the giant Dallas mall, Conner disappeared. He was wearing a bright-orange shirt and had striking sun-bleached blond hair, yet he just vanished from everyone's sight. An hour passed, and I had to make the most difficult call of my life to tell my husband that our son could not be found.

No one wants to make that call. No one wants to *get* that call.

The store had been shut down and locked, and every clerk was looking for him. The police were called. A solid hour after he had been lost, one of the staff in Banana Republic heard a little movement. They pushed back the clothing and found Conner hiding between a wall and a rack of pants. By the time I found our son, he was crying. I wanted to kill him. But I've never been happier to see anyone in my life.

He was crying because that entire time he heard us looking for him and screaming his name, all he could think was that he was going to get in trouble. So he didn't speak. He sat there terrified, hiding behind the pants in Banana Republic.

Maybe you are well versed in hiding behind the pants. You'd rather sit there quietly with all your emotions and feelings tucked inside than risk them coming out if you face the gravity and reality that awaits you. So you stay glued to the wall. And yet it does not change the fact that circumstances are waiting for you that must be confronted and that will not go away just because you hide behind the pants. In fact, the more time that goes by, the more desperate, chaotic, and needy your realities become.

Please hear me: **You don't have to tell *everyone*; you have to tell *someone*.**

I know the damage that can flow out of a reaction to our emotions; I know the *beauty* they can catalyze too. Emotions are tools. Which means that whenever we feel an emotion, we can use that feeling to spur us on toward God, or we can use it to sit there and sin.

Here's what we can't do if we want to live healthy and free: We can't stuff the thing and just move on.

I think of my son who gets in the car after the turbulence of middle school. Some days he explodes and tells me every hard thing about his day and we go to McDonald's and get a shake and cheeseburger and by four o'clock he is laughing. And on some days, he holds it in, maybe because of shame or just sheer exhaustion, and by dinner he is exploding on one of us.

It's exhausting how much energy we burn trying to keep our box of emotions hidden and neatly out of view. And even with all that effort, stuffed emotions inevitably find their way out, oftentimes sideways on the people we love.

Boxes stuffed with feelings can't stay closed forever.

I'll say it again: You don't have to tell *everyone*; you have to tell *someone*.

How are you really? The skilled concealers love the word *fine*. It is the greatest rug to lay out over all the unsightly places in our lives. *Fine* is short and grammatically correct and leads to very few additional questions. But it also doesn't do a single thing to help sort out that tangle of emotions you've stuffed into a box in the corner of your heart.

As an example of how the strategy of concealing our emotions can affect your soul and your body—all of you—my son-in-law,

Charlie, graciously gave me permission to tell you about his going to therapy for the first time in his entire life.

Charlie is a guy who has always been fine. He's super easygoing, not easily revved up by circumstances, the kind of person who takes things as they come and whose internal motor runs smoothly almost seven days a week.

But some stuff has been coming up for Charlie recently, stuff that he thought he should address. The collective suggestion from his friends and family sounded something like, "We're going to pray for you. Have you talked to a doctor about how you're feeling? What about therapy? Have you ever been to therapy?"

He got the message.

So, Charlie went to therapy for his first time. And when he got home, he proceeded to take a five-hour nap.

In the middle of the afternoon.

When he later told the rest of us what had happened, we all laughed together with him. Because we had all been there before too.

And then guess what Charlie did? He made another appointment with that therapist. After that next meeting, he called and booked him again.

And again. And again. And again.

Once he got on his feet emotionally, he started telling his friends about how much better and clearer he felt. He started having deeper, more substantive conversations with those guys, listening to them more intently and kindly than many of them had ever experienced in their lives.

As he started to heal, he began to bring healing to others.

This is how it goes.

. . .

IT'S HARD TO unlearn the patterns that have been ingrained in us. But if we choose the easiest paths every time, if we check out through controlling and coping and concealing, we miss the best parts of life. The parts we are actually craving.

Because there is a better way to respond to emotions: fully embracing the purpose they were made for—connection. Connection to God and connection to others.

6

CREATED TO CONNECT

Have you ever sat down with someone for coffee or lunch and that person started sharing what was really going on in their life, maybe even getting teary about it?

How do you feel in that moment? Sure, there might be a moment or two of awkwardness, but beneath the uncertainty of what to say or do, what is it that you feel?

I bet you feel compassion.

Affection.

Grateful, even, that they shared their life with you.

You feel *connected* to them, even if you don't know them all that well. That's what emotions are meant to do: connect us to what is most important. And to who is most important.

Our emotions have a purpose, and that purpose is to connect us to God and one another.

THE ROPE CONNECTING US TO GOD

Everything that God has placed inside us is for the purpose of drawing us near to Him, to trust Him. Take away the childlike fear and we lose our childlike inclination to pull close and ask

Him for help. Take away excitement at an incredible meal and we lose our awe and wonder at the gifts of God. Take away hope and we never look to heaven. Take away peace and we never rest in God.

The truth that sets us free begins with the truth that we are sad or hurting and desperately and urgently need help. There is no hope for health, joy, peace, and salvation apart from Jesus, the One who is all and has done all for us. He died on the cross for our sins. He was raised to new life again. He offers us grace and forgiveness and an eternity spent with Him.

That's it.

That's the gospel.

The Bible is clear that the truth of that sets us free:

> Jesus said to the Jews who had believed him, "If you abide in my word, you are truly my disciples, and you will know the truth, and the truth will set you free. . . . So if the Son sets you free, you will be free indeed."[1]

Certainly, Jesus is speaking of Himself in this verse: the truth of who He is as the means and the way of salvation. The ultimate freedom we need is to be freed from the eternal consequences of our sin. And right now, that is available to you if you trust Jesus as the only means for salvation.

But it doesn't stop there. The Bible is filled with stories of people who worked out that hope and truth and freedom with their emotions, with how they felt.

Paul hated Christians, was murdering them, until Christ met him and rescued him. That extreme emotion turned to impassioned grace and fervor to reach the world with the hope of Jesus.[2]

King David poured out his guts throughout the book of Psalms. The songs of lament are the most emotive, raw, messy parts of the Bible. He's mad at God. He's sad with God. He has given up and lost all hope, and then, in his honesty with God and himself and others who are listening, he comes back to all that he knows to be good and true of God.

The beauty of David and the Psalms is the permission to feel it all. David had full confidence that God could handle all his emotions, even the ones that caused him to doubt that God is good and that God still loves him. He sees injustice go unpunished and he's ticked!

He feels safe enough with God to wrestle it all out! Do you?

THE TRUTH? IT is freeing. It's freeing when we tell the truth! But we can't get that done without admitting how we feel, without confessing what our lived experience is.

We can confess sin.

We can share our pain.

We can confide our fears.

We can cry through gut-wrenching grief.

We get to express what we're thinking as long as we express what we're feeling too. Tell God and trusted loved ones all these things so that you can finally live fully free, connected to one another by the rope of emotion.

IF, AS YOU'RE reading these words, you're feeling paralyzed by sadness, anger, grief, or disappointment, I want you to know something: Given everything we are presented with in this lovely world of ours, it's amazing to me that you don't feel *more* than what you're feeling right now. That's the first thing I would say, were we seated across from each other, face-to-face.

We know that emotions are all-encompassing. They make you ecstatic when you see your kids succeed on their own and take their first steps. They make you feel sick to your stomach when you're nervous and scared. They make you feel your chest get tight when you're reminded that the future is beyond your control. They make you anxious when you fall in love and aren't sure the other person feels the same way. They make you cry when you see pain and suffering and can't fix it in your life or in the world. Something about emotions is connected to our thoughts, but equally true is that they're also different somehow.

Maybe you feel like you are staring at an ocean of emotions, wondering how you could ever get across. It's too big. All the hope and grief, joy and anxiety, unshakable memories both good and painful. How on earth do you cross? And then closing in behind you is life, the constant reality of the people needing to eat, the assignments that are due, the places you need to be.

How am I supposed to deal with this ocean?

Do I even want to do this right now?

I'm here to remind you that you are not standing on that shore alone. The same God who accompanied the Israelites as they stared at the water in front of them, knowing the Egyptians were closing in from behind, and the same God who split the sea—He split the sea!—that God is near. He's right there beside you. He can do a miracle here.

The war lies at this crossroads.

In case this is news to you, I hate to be the one to tell you that as believers in Jesus Christ, we have an enemy. A serious enemy. An enemy who wants to take us down.

The goal of that enemy is to create chaos and division. And when it comes to this topic in our own hearts and as we survey our homes and friendships and just the whole world, the Enemy seems to be succeeding. The emotional landscape feels chaotic and divided.

So we shut down.

We want to escape because everything feels too big and too hard and we feel ill-equipped.

It reminds me of when Zac rented an itty-bitty boat one time on a vacation. He took me out on the open sea in a boat the size of a dining table. Which would have been lovely, were it not for the waves being bigger than our boat. We almost died. For real. Even my never-flustered husband tugged his little orange life preserver on.

The point: We were not equipped.

It's not supposed to be this way.

I think of Moses, when God through the burning bush is calling him to obey in a big way. He's afraid and he's confused and he feels all kinds of emotions and inadequacy. God does not comfort him by telling him that the circumstances will be easy or doable; He comforts him by reminding Moses who He is. He says to him, "I AM WHO I AM."[3]

I AM before there was time.

I AM after the story of earth is over.

I AM safe for all the fears.

I AM enough to conquer them.

I AM not going anywhere.

I AM already in the future.

I AM the holder of every thought that you think.

I AM the holder of the universe.

I AM not thwarted by the Enemy's schemes.

I AM planning things you couldn't imagine for your future.

I AM in the days of rejoicing at a birth.

I AM holding you on the day you bury the one you love.

Our ultimate security rests wholly and completely on who God is. He is why we're okay. He is also why we can be broken and doubt and fear and cry.

We think God is waiting for us to pull ourselves together, but actually He is waiting for us to come to Him and fall apart.

The more I do this, the more I heal.

The more I don't do this with God and others, the more anxiety and depression grow in me.

And that's true for you too.

Jesus said, "Unless you change and become like little children, you will never enter the kingdom of heaven."[4]

He was speaking to the know-it-alls, to the people leading with their heads rather than their hearts. He was speaking to the ones who saw their lives as performances to be rewarded rather than relationships.

We need to become kids again with God. Needy. Honest. Crying if we need to cry.

Jesus says in the Sermon on the Mount, "Blessed are those who mourn, for they shall be comforted."[5]

People are more blessed if they mourn because they get God in a state that the trying-only-to-be-happy people don't. They get Him saying, "Come here. I have you. I want to be with you in this, kid."

Maybe you slipped into postpartum depression after delivering one of your babies. . . .

Maybe you wrestled for years on the heels of losing a loved one. . . .

Maybe you've had rounds and rounds of medical tests and still can't figure out what is wrong. . . .

Whatever situation has left you tangled up in your feelings, God is saying, "I am on the other side of this rope. Lay down the controlling, coping, and hiding and just come say it all. Come feel it all. I got you. I want to have you."

Emotions are the gifts that connect it all. Us to ourselves. Us to God. Us to one another.

"Blessed are those who mourn." We get more of God and more of one another—if we open up our hearts to it.

WHAT GOD WANTS FOR YOU

I want to pause here just a moment and give you space to exhale. I want you to feel the tremendous compassion I have for you as you consider the ways you have dealt with your emotions in the past and the way you may feel tangled up in them right now. I want to say again, of course. Of course you have controlled and coped and tried to conceal it. Of course you have at times acted all kinds of wrong ways and even lashed out at God because of overwhelming emotions. Of course! Because it all is so much! You have had to carry more hurt than should ever be carried. So, of course it's easier to try to control, cope, or conceal it. Of course you sometimes crumble under the weight of it all.

Of course you do. We all do.

Because it's all too much.

And guess what? "We do not have a high priest who is unable to sympathize with our weaknesses, but one who in every respect has been tempted as we are, yet without sin," so, the writer of Hebrews continues, "let us then with confidence draw near to the throne of grace, that we may receive mercy and find grace to help in time of need."[6]

Jesus is going to help us do this. My dream for this book is that you would feel like I was walking beside you and pointing to Jesus, who is walking beside us and giving us small steps to feel again and to heal. He is doing that, you know.

I believe He is doing exactly that.

If you follow Jesus, then you have been given a new heart. The Holy Spirit is with you and in you and issuing you the ability to love with the feelings that used to only lead you to selfishness.

We keep needing God. We need Him to walk with us through all of it, as we talk to Him, asking Him what we must know and must do. Every feeling should be felt and taken straight to Scripture and Jesus. Every feeling ought to prompt us to ask God, "What should I do?"

Jeremiah 17:9, the verse mentioned earlier and so often quoted to remind us that the heart is deceitful, was never meant to void the gift of our feelings. It is a reminder that we need God in the midst of them. We need truth in the midst of our feelings.

Jesus said of Himself,

The Spirit of the Lord is on me,
>   because he has anointed me
>   to proclaim good news to the poor.

He has sent me to proclaim freedom for the prisoners
>   and recovery of sight for the blind,
> to set the oppressed free,
>   to proclaim the year of the Lord's favor.[7]

That freedom is a promise not just for heaven but also for your soul today, and that freedom comes as you face the truth. All of it in you and around you.

What is true?

The psalmist David wrote of God, "Behold, You desire truth in the innermost being, and in secret You will make wisdom known to me."[8] This is what God wants for you: wisdom and truth, not just in your brain, heart, and body, but *in your innermost being,* healing your soul to the depth of who you are and why you're here.

God built us mind, body, and soul. He wrapped us in flesh and set us here at this time and in this space, and **the mystery of what we feel and how we experience it all points to a God who not only built our emotions but feels every last one of them too.**

THE ROPE CONNECTING US TO ONE ANOTHER

Connection with God is not the only gift we find when we get honest about our emotions.

Back when I was stuck in that totally numb state that initially propelled me into this journey to better understand my emotions, I asked a therapist I'd met during a group session if I could meet with him one-on-one. At the time, I was halfway through a sabbatical I'd taken to try to recover from burnout. I'm not even sure I can put words to what I was going through at the time, but the overall sensation was that of feeling pressured. I had been running so fast for so long that it was like my life was on auto-pilot. My achiever side just kept showing up, digging in, trying to play the game without anyone noticing that I wasn't there at all. I was sinking. It was July, and I was due to head back to work in August, but every time I thought about that return, my heart raced, my mind whirled, and I just felt overwhelmed to the point of panic.

The biggest calling on my life was now eliciting horror, anxiety, and dread.

I explained all this to Dr. C, as I call him, on our video call after he asked what he needed to know about how I was *really* doing. Which is when he gave me this astounding advice . . .

Oh wait, he gave me no advice at all. Instead, here is what Dr. C did: He listened. He listened well. He asked thoughtful questions. He told me it was understandable that I felt like I felt.

He then said something I won't forget for a long, long time: "Jennie, I know you're stressed and frustrated, and I want you to know that I will never tire of hearing you say how you really feel. I'm not leaving the room." Of course, it was a metaphorical room since we were on Zoom, but I knew what he meant.

I'm not leaving the room.

Isn't that what we're afraid of? That we feel our feelings and work up the courage to say them, and the person or people we entrusted them to will quietly back up and slip out of the door to escape the mess of it?

Here's what I know: I went into that video call feeling like my ministry was about to fall apart, not because God wasn't blessing it but because I could no longer find the strength to lead within it.

And I came out of that session feeling as though I could breathe again, all because someone across from me didn't try to fix it. They listened and stayed.

The weight I'd been carrying had somehow miraculously lifted. Now, I had been working through this for upwards of a year in group therapy. But I walked into the kitchen to get something to eat after that call thinking, *What in the world just happened? How can I feel so much better now?*

Later, when I asked what kind of magic he had worked to alleviate the anxiety I had felt for so long, Dr. C told me, "There was nothing magical about it, really. You just no longer feel alone."

IN LOVE, GOD created you, created all people, and set us here.

He imagined walking with us and talking with us and helping us through this life.

He wanted a relationship with us.

Not only that but He wanted us to have each other, just like He was in relationship with Himself—Father, Son, Spirit. He saw a man and knew it was "not good" for him to be alone.[9]

So He gave us each other.

So that we could walk with each other on this planet.

So that we could walk with each other as we walk with Him. Together.

Then sin came and it all broke. But His plan would be accomplished. His plan never changed.

Jesus came to reconcile us back to God and back to one another.

Yet here we are, still acting like we don't need God, like we don't need one another.

THE HARD. THE grief. The ecstatic joy. The fear. The anger. It was all meant to drive us to God and to need each other.

Because **the point of life is** *connection*—**with God, with our own hearts, and with the people God puts in our distinctive corner of the world.**

And the way we find and maintain those connections is by feeling the feelings we're feeling and inviting others to do the same with theirs. In the words of Dr. Curt Thompson, "To live in the way of love requires that I pay attention to the fact that my mind, through the process of emotion, longs to be connected to others."[10]

Connection is why we're here.

BEING EMOTIONALLY PRESENT, FOR OURSELVES AND OTHERS

Connection is the greatest gift we have in life. Connection to our own selves. Connection to each other. Connection with God.

Which explains why the greatest strategy our enemy employs against us is to *disconnect* us from those things. And one of the ways he accomplishes this is to manipulate, distract, and confuse.

As it relates to our emotions then, Satan has a heyday.

Take the situation with Kate: If I hadn't recently been learning about how to deal with my feelings as they arose, I can guarantee that upon being triggered by my daughter telling me she might be moving, I would have reached unapologetically for *control.*

And as I worked to control my emotions, that dysfunction would morph into trying to control Kate.

I could have sulked around our relationship for months— years?—refusing to celebrate *anything* in her life. I could have demonstrated through my words and actions that I cared far more about this circumstance of her maybe moving than about the relationship that she and I share.

When I was busy freaking out over Kate's hypothetical departure, I couldn't be present to hear her dreams.

When I was holed away in my bedroom, tears streaming down my cheeks, I couldn't respond to the bid for connection she was extending to me by trusting me with those dreams.

I could go on, but you get the idea:

We can't be present with God and others when we're refusing to be present with ourselves. Which is why I'm writing this book for us, to teach us how to do just that.

We can't be emotionally healthy if we refuse to be emotionally honest.

We all are craving healthy, deep relationships. Vulnerability and safety pave the road to that goal. To be seen, soothed, and safe are things we all came out of the womb craving, and that can't exist without emotions being shared. We express them, and we hold them for others.

My recent counseling journey with Dr. C actually began when my feisty friend Jessica texted a bunch of her friends—me included—and said, "Guys, we need to get together intentionally and frequently so we aren't alone in all the stress we are carrying."

She wanted us to do a three-hour call every month and a three-day retreat once a year—that was the commitment we'd be making if we said yes to this cohort of friends. And she invited Dr. C to be our counselor.

I needed this. I'd been angst-ridden at work for months, maybe years. Ten years prior, my little living-room Bible study had inadvertently exploded into public ministry, a lot of it. As I mentioned earlier, I found myself leading a growing ministry, IF:Gathering, which should have felt like the greatest joy of my life. But I was close to burnout, and I didn't totally know why. I loved the work I did, but the pressure was drowning me. I needed people who understood and people who could help me understand what was wrong.

Honestly, I wanted people to fix me. That's what I was hoping for.

I texted Jess back: *I'm in.*

At the retreat center, during our group's in-person gathering, I exhaled. I took in the expectant faces staring back at me, each one belonging to a dear friend, most of whom I'd known for a decade—truly, these were women I admired and adored.

Dr. C was our facilitator. And because he and I had met before in similar circumstances years earlier, I knew this experience would demand of me a full-on lay down of what I was feeling and why. Which is always awkward for me. Add to the mix the fact that these friends are among the many who know I'm not good at feeling, and my stress was pretty much sky-high. But I'd come ready. I would impress them with my feelings. I would have feelings. I would have feelings about my feelings. I would share all the feelings I had.

I was second to speak. I shared story after story of hurt and rejection and disappointment with people, with work, with my life. Through tears, I clenched my fists and said with great passion, "I'm mad. I'm mad at God. I feel like He has used me and called me so far out on the ocean of risk, and at times it feels like He has abandoned me. I am sick of the pressure, and I don't want to do this anymore, but I still love Him and don't want to disappoint Him. And all this makes me feel stuck."

I was now bawling, the kind of crying where you can't keep talking even if you wanted to, the kind that makes your breath do weird things and makes the other people's eyes get wide.

"I hate . . . this," I stuttered out eventually. "I am . . . so [sob, sob] tired. So worn . . . out. So . . . frustrated . . . and angry and . . . [more sobbing] sad."

I was mad.

I was *mad* mad. I felt used up and spat out by God, and I was finally admitting it.

Eventually, a voice broke through my weeping. "God isn't like that."

"I know you're hurting," another voice said, "but, Jennie, this just isn't true."

"Something else just has to be going on," a third voice all but whispered. "I don't think God would do that to you."

My anger turned to rage. How could I be so misunderstood by these friends?

I was ready to bolt, in classic Jennie style. Go in, do what I'm supposed to do, and get out of there. I thought I'd understood the assignment. I'd been as real as it gets. I'd shown up with every pent-up feeling I'd been living with, and now I felt miserable and judged for it.

Another person spoke up, the sole guy in the room, our fearless brilliant leader, Dr. C. "Jennie, how do you feel about what everyone is sharing with you?"

At this moment, I had a choice: I could play it cool—some nice things had been said in between all the judgy things, and I could just choose to focus on those. Or I could show them how angry and hurt I was. I could tell them how I really felt.

Breaking into that awkward silence when nobody really knows what to say or do, I snapped, "Honestly, I'm ticked. I just shared all my hurts, and you guys made me feel like I shouldn't feel that way. And maybe you're right. But I do feel this way. And I thought it was safe to say it. But now I feel like you are defending God and looking for where I went wrong."

Dr. C smiled, pleased by my bravery, as my friends scrambled.

Someone—Melissa, maybe, or Ann?—spoke up. "I feel . . . sad . . . that you feel misunderstood by us," she said. "I really am. I'm sad that you feel judged and shamed."

With those simple words "I feel," something decompressed in my knotted-up soul. Something that had felt misunderstood.

The rest of the group nodded along with their statements. They apologized. They said they felt proud of me for continuing to obey God even when I was so mad, for persevering and for being honest with them.

I felt safe again. I felt seen. I felt comforted. I went from feeling angry and misunderstood to feeling profoundly close to women who had hurt me moments before. And the wild irony is that in articulating that I was mad at God, I no longer felt so mad at Him. And I didn't feel so alone in it all.

"Your tendency is always going to be to try to fix each another," Dr. C said, "because you're problem solvers at your core." Instead of trying to fix one another, Dr. C wanted us to feel. With that as his motivation, he set some ground rules for our time together.

Listen intently.

Listen fully.

Only respond with "I feel . . . ," not "I think."

If someone besides me had been on the mat weeping when Dr. C set these rules, I wouldn't have understood how the guidelines could have helped. I would have been cynical, thinking, *No. People need perspective. People need to get their beliefs right. People need to know truth. These are the things that help people, the things that fix people.*

But I had just experienced something new. There had been a complete shift in the room, and in my soul, all because people shifted from saying what they thought about me and my problems to telling me how they felt.

So, I was all in on this journey Dr. C was calling us to. It was a whole new way of life. A new way of feeling my feelings. Yes, it was messy, even scary, but it was the beginning of something that has changed me. *I feel.* I really feel today. I feel all the feelings with my people and because of them. I am not all fixed, but I am changed because today I am at home in my own soul with God and with others.

And that healing has set me free in so many areas. I can now hold my kid who is crying and not rush to make them stop. I can hold my friend's grief and not rush to make it go away. I can sit with my own tears and let them fall, and I can run to Jesus and call a friend in the middle of my cry. I can celebrate and dance and laugh when life is good, because my heart is awake and safe and seen.

My once-tangled ropes are now straight and smooth, lifelines connecting me to God and the people I love. And in all this, I've really discovered so much more of the abundant whole life Jesus promised we could have.

And I want this for you too. I want you to be able to stop controlling, coping, and concealing and see how the best parts of life show up when we vulnerably, bravely untangle that rope with our God and our people.

7

A VISION FOR
SOMETHING BETTER

Before we start working through the actual process involved in feeling our feelings, I have a question for you: When you consider your emotional life, what is it that you want?

This is a visioning question, a question of aspiration, of longing, of dreams. And it's important to begin here because it's something we don't often think about.

Maybe you want to be more wholehearted and feel more deeply so you can connect with your family or friends with more compassion. Or maybe you want to heal the bitterness you can't seem to let go of. Or maybe you want to hope again and quit feeling so sad every day.

Or maybe you are tired of feeling so many wild feelings and you just want peace. You feel so much and need to know what to do with it all, and the tangles have you stuck and angry at the world or just so sad you don't want to keep going, or it all keeps coming out sideways and hurting people you love by accident.

All of it. I get it.

I honestly get all of it. And I'm telling you: There is hope for this all.

Here's what I've been learning as I've been working to defrost my numbed-out state: Rather than shaming ourselves for the emotions we're feeling (or choosing *not* to feel, as the case may be), we can survey the world around us, look ourselves squarely in the eye, and say, "Of *course* you feel this way."

Listen, the world is *wild*. Of course we feel wild emotions!

If we've met in previous books of mine, then you know that I'm a raving fan of John Bunyan's stellar classic *The Pilgrim's Progress*. I love that book so much because it displays the mess of the Christian walk. The main character, not so subtly named Christian, begins to trust Jesus early in his journey, even as he keeps falling into pits of despair, becoming locked up in fear and doubt, and being distracted by the ways of the world. It's so relatable. After all, **where did those of us who know Jesus get the idea that we were going to have a straight and easy path all the way to heaven?** It's a wild ride *all* the way home.

And we will need God and we will need each other if we ever hope to survive. But isn't that the point? All the posturing and pretending we have picked up because we aren't supposed to feel our feelings or give too much attention to them—what a crock. Our feelings often tell us something true.

It's our feelings that tell us something is broken.

It's our feelings that tell us something is hurt.

It's our feelings that tell us we need God's assistance.

It's our feelings that tell us we're alive.

Even if you weren't overtly harmed as a child, you haven't exactly skated by. Our experience on this planet is far from perfect—

it's true for everyone. Which is why it's not only acceptable to feel mixed-up emotions, but it's actually as it should be.

Why? Because the more we let ourselves feel all the feelings we're truly feeling, the more we are freed to love and create with all that energy we tend to burn trying to keep those feelings at bay.

We all make messes—every one of us.

But **amid the mess, our emotions can also light the way to undeniable beauty.**

A MAGNIFICENT MESS

I want to lay out a scenario that happened in my life just three days ago, to show you that having a lofty vision for our emotional lives is absolutely worth it, that it's actually attainable, and that even a recovering fixer like me can aspire to emotional success.

You ready?

Here goes.

Three days ago, I was standing in the middle of our house, and my kids were all there and ten thousand of their friends. And I wanted to scream at the top of my lungs because Zac Allen had made me furious. Zac and I have gotten pretty good at navigating the inevitable turmoil of family life, but we're not perfect.

On this particular night, he had lost his temper, a kid had lost their temper, and I was about to lose mine. Now, this would have been embarrassing because the house was *full* of kids who are close to being my own but not quite. And we were having a lovely night of Rummikub and tacos. I withdrew to my room and began to cry. And while I can't go into every detail about what this fight was about because it involves people and details that are not mine to share, I can say that this angry feeling was really a feeling of being hurt.

I felt betrayed.

I felt unseen.

I felt as though the people who love me the most were hurting me the most.

Why start with this story? Because it was this past Thursday night. As in, while I was writing this book about healthy ways to feel our feelings.

I don't anticipate a future for any of us where all our emotions are perfectly tucked into the right spaces in our bodies and minds, perfectly in control, perfectly expressed, and perfectly understood. I think it's important to start with some honesty about that. I don't want to overpromise and underdeliver.

But let me tell you what unfolded since Thursday that I believe could unfold for you as we journey together.

Thursday night, I cried myself to sleep. I hadn't cried in a few months. I hadn't been this mad in a few years. And I was neck-deep in my research and discovery about God's plan for our emotions. What was I going to do now that was different than how I would've responded before all this?

Friday morning came and I still was teary, and I met with God in my sadness and even in my anger. I wasn't afraid of any of it. I just told Him exactly what I felt, exactly what I feared, and exactly what I was thinking. I didn't clean it all up or pretend that it was all okay; I just cried out to Him in all the chaos.

I pulled my kid that had been in the middle of this mess close and said, "Do you want to be sad with me?" He said no, but he stayed in the room anyway. And by the time he left, he had tears and we felt closer than ever.

Instead of withdrawing from my husband and pouting for days like I might have in the early years, I pulled him close too. I expressed with my words exactly how I had been hurt and how I felt misunderstood. Somehow in that mess, we felt closer than ever too.

This isn't some magical, mystical journey we're about to take.

We're going to look at realistic ways to be more emotionally healthy.

Do you believe you could be emotionally free and healthy? Do you believe that?

We can untangle our emotions and chart a path out of our pain.

I promise you, we can.

But I also promise that the path won't always be easy.

FEELING OUR WAY IN THE DARK

Before we move into the next section, I want to get really clear about an important topic. There is a crucial difference between being tangled up in your emotions and suffering from clinical depression or anxiety. I firmly believe the process we're about to walk through can help absolutely anyone move toward emotional health, but I just as firmly believe that sometimes medicine and therapy are necessary.

If you're wrestling in this way, I want you to know I'm just so sorry. You've been on my mind through all these words because as I have been writing these words, the person I love the most on earth has been fighting depression and anxiety right beside me.

And I know from intimate experience with depression how necessary it is that we address this before we go any further.

I've shared glimpses of this part of Zac's and my story before, but still today it's difficult for me to get my mind around the fact that this actually happened to us. Early in our marriage, after Zac and I launched and grew a church plant in Austin and then handed it off to new leadership, my husband hit a brick wall. I remember his preaching his last sermon and then, as if on cue, falling into a deep, dark depression. Regarding that time, he said, "I never once contemplated committing suicide, but I certainly came to understand why people do." He says the depression lasted nine months; my recollection is that it was more than a year. Either way, the duration was far too long for us both.

When I tell you that I lost my husband that year, it's no exaggeration. Zac would be in the room physically, while emotionally he was miles away. He was just . . . gone. Glazed over. Unfeeling. Disengaged. Apathetic to all that was happening or not happening in the life of our family—with the kids, with me, with us all.

We'd adopted a toddler, and my ministry was growing around that same time. And during so many sleepless nights, I wondered how in the world I was going to make it to the next morning and how I'd cope with the day from there. It was like being haunted by a ghost who happens to sleep in the same bed as you.

Zac set a few goals for himself most days: Get out of bed, get to the gym, take a shower, and eat something if he could. But in terms of interacting with any other human being in any sort of meaningful way, that was a bridge too far. He would later tell me that it felt like he was lying at the bottom of the ocean, looking up at the sun-kissed surface of the water, miles and miles above his head. He could see the lighted edge. He wanted to get to the lighted edge. He just had no clue how to resurface. And so there he lay, unsmiling, unmoving, depressed.

One of the pastors at our church at the time, named Kevin, told Zac that everything would be okay. He told Zac that the depression wouldn't last forever, that at some point he'd reemerge. Of course, Kevin had no real way of knowing that to be true, but he had walked a dozen pastors through depression before, so we chose to believe his assessment of things. Plus, what else were we supposed to do?

Thankfully, Kevin wound up being right, and one day it was like my beloved husband returned from a yearlong trip to somewhere far, far away. He was back in all his Zac-ness: smiling, laughing, engaging, ministering, serving, loving everyone so well. We exhaled. Now we could move ahead.

All this happened so long ago that it feels like I'm speaking of a different lifetime. Which is why it was so disorienting when, just about the time I decided to write this book, I started noticing that Zac, once again, was off.

For the past few years, Zac has been working to build something that both satisfies his entrepreneurial hunger and provides for our family. He poured countless hours into the organization and sustainability of this business by planning, strategizing, managing, and accounting for every aspect of the company. But things were falling apart, and the idea that it was now all going away was causing him a level of stress, anxiety, and pain I'd not seen in him for a long, long time.

He was saying all the right things in response to the questions I was asking:

. . .

Is your identity wrapped up in your work?
No.

Are you mad at God?
No.

Are you comparing yourself to other people?
No, no. Not at all.

Zac wasn't having an identity crisis. He wasn't in the throes of a spiritual takedown with God. He wasn't questioning his worth as a husband or dad. His thoughts were in order. He was believing truth about God and himself and even held tightly to hope that in the end we would be okay.

The truth of the matter, he said, was simply that *he was sad.*

Zac was seemingly at ease in this emotion. Not surprisingly, I wanted it gone. *No!* I initially thought. *We have to fix this. Sad. We've already done sad. Lord, what if this pit is as deep and dark as the first one? What if he slips further? Disappears?*

I had a decision to make upon hearing those words from Zac. He did too, actually: Would we allow time and space for his sadness, or would we wrestle that thing to the ground? I don't think we overtly talked about our strategy then, but what seemed to occur to us simultaneously was that he needed to walk *through* this thing. *We* needed to walk through this thing.

There are times in life when we can't go over something or under something or around something. We simply have to walk through it.

Listen, I know that God has given us power over our thoughts, but God also has given us the gift of emotions. And something about this moment wasn't about what Zac was thinking; it was about what he was feeling. Feelings he needed to feel. Now, in these months, he has also visited a counselor, pulled in close community and shared everything, and even revisited meds that in the past played a role in stabilizing him. I have watched him live everything so beautifully that I am about to share with you.

He's named it and shared it and sat with it, and it has drawn him closer to all of us and to Jesus.

But what I know now—or at least am learning—that I was clueless about years ago is that Zac's situation isn't something to fix. It's something we've got to feel our way through.

"We're going to be okay," I say to him ten or twelve times each day.

To which he replies, "This isn't gonna last forever."

We *will* make it through—I know we will.

We're going to be okay. I think.

The night Zac shared with our kids the place he was in emotionally and the realities of the state of the business, our oldest grown son sent him these words:

Dad, sitting here just crying and thinking about what you're going through. I know you're asleep, and I'll tell you in person, but I want you to know I'm so proud of the father and the businessman that you have been for me and taught me to be.

I see your work ethic, vision, and execution every day, and it breaks my heart to see a dream not come to fruition. But all I can think about amidst grieving with you is how proud I am that you're my dad. I don't think I'd be crying if I didn't love you and think of you as a best friend. That alone is something I will continually pray for with my future son. I love you, Dad, and I know I don't tell you enough, but I'm so proud of you and will follow you into battle anywhere! If you and Mom need anything out of me, I'll be there. Thank you for dinner tonight.

In the dark night, some of the greatest moments of life are found. But Zac would miss things like this if he pretended he was okay. He isn't, but we will be together as we go.

If our story feels similar to your own story, whether bouts or a constant fight with paralyzing anxiety or depression, I pray and believe you'll make it through as you remember that God is there in the valley with you, just as He promises.[1]

And I hope the words in the pages to come give you a vision for a way through the dark night as well. Let's feel our way through together.

FINDING A WAY FORWARD

When I was on that Zoom call with Dr. C, what I needed wasn't a pep talk about how everything would be okay at work. What I needed was to know that in my overwhelmed panic, I wasn't alone.

When I was at that retreat with my cohort friends, what I needed wasn't judgment for being angry at God. What I needed was to know that in my anger, I wasn't alone.

Once your brain and heart realize that you aren't alone, your muscles can quit clenching and your heart can open back up.

We can live in meaningful connection with others—with God, with our own hearts, with the people God puts in our path. I will show you the steps of noticing and naming and feeling and sharing our feelings, and also getting help when we need it. And while it's tempting for me to blast through that progression with lightning-fast speed, I've intentionally built this next section of the book with each stage occupying its very own chapter.

I want to break down what we actually can do with our feelings so that, whether you feel a million different things jumbled up or you wonder if your emotions aren't there because you haven't felt in so long, you will have something simple to do that helps anyone starting from anyplace untangle it one step at a time.

The knots of our souls untangle with a few moves, and I am going to lead you through each one. And although the process isn't what I would call easy, it will help us live at ease a little more, day by day.

Before we dive into that process, I want to give you a vision for what is about to happen.

My friend Caroline is midwestern too and rarely fazed by anything. In fact, she runs our events at IF:Gathering like she's hosting a baby shower instead of planning the biggest women's event on earth.

Recently, she was staying with my kids and—shocker—they completely wore her out and sent her into a bit of a spin. Now, I want to use Caroline as an example because she is a really emotionally steady person. You remember my canoe analogy? She doesn't hit the bank often. Caroline has a wide river, with not a lot of trauma in her story. She is largely able to communicate her emotions in real time and stay in the middle of the river. But apparently my kids have the ability to take the greatest canoers and ram them into the side of the bank.

Details aside, my kids plus a lot of other stress sent Caroline into a panic over something that normally wouldn't bother her. She told me later her paralysis was a reaction to a lot of things out of her control and that what she really needed in that moment was help. She needed someone else to step in and make decisions and organize the day and help everyone survive. She had read a first draft of this book, so she didn't overthink her wave of emotion. She felt it. She named it and she called out—in this case, she asked her husband to come over. She couldn't calm herself down, but he could be in the crazy with her.

All of us need that sometimes. Someone to help regulate us when we can't regulate ourselves.

When I asked her if this process we did together helped in that moment, if it worked, she giggled and said, "Yes, it did! Noticing it, naming it, feeling it, and calling for help in the midst of it . . . worked!"

Zac Allen is a great canoer—in real life, I mean. He doesn't just think he's a great canoer; he actually is one. The only way I ever make it down the river is by doing exactly what he says.

I mention this because sometimes the greatest regulation for our emotions is having someone beside us, getting us out of bed, reminding us to move our body, meet with Jesus, and get dressed. If you're single, that might feel like a cruel statement. But I believe in community so close and deep that your people could do that for you—maybe even better than a spouse. So often, it is my closest friends doing this for me.

Bottom line: What we are about to do together will change

you, stretch you, and bring you life, but you need your people. If your answer to that is, "I don't have my people," then mark your spot in this book, set it down, and go read my book *Find Your People*. You need people in the boat with you!

All right. It's time. Let's do this.

how to untangle our insides

8

GETTING PAST *FINE*

NOTICE
NAME
FEEL
SHARE
CHOOSE

The other night, I was making dinner for my family, when I started getting what I can only describe as an itchy feeling in my mind and soul. Have you ever had this happen? You're busy doing something. There are other people in the room. You think you're hanging in there, being normal, living life. But something keeps bugging you, something down deep in the recesses of your being. You can't pinpoint it exactly, but you're aware that it's there. Do you push past it and keep doing what you're doing, or do you slow down and take it in?

That's where I was that night, right at that fork in the road. I just wanted to finish making the meal and get dinner on the table. But then there was this fly buzzing through my brain that seemingly wouldn't be silenced until I gave it a swat or two.

Standing at the stove, I stopped stirring. I shut my eyes just for a second to block out the scene unfolding all around me. For a moment, I ignored the one kid who was lamenting a significant-other challenge, the other kid who evidently needed money for something and was busy laying out a bulletproof case, and the husband who was inadvertently exasperated with both kids, prompting me to keep jumping in as referee.

I considered my options:

I could pour a glass of wine.

I could blow past all this, plop dinner on the table, and go to bed.

I could holler, "Guys, I can't take any more of this crap! Everyone just stop—*now*."

Or I could do this differently.

Here's the funny thing about those first three options: We think that when we control, cope, or conceal, we've somehow managed the feelings we feel. This couldn't be further from the truth. When we distract ourselves from how we're feeling or stuff down the emotions that are begging for breath or demand that our circumstances and the people within them somehow change to conform to our whims, we've only kicked the problem up the path a few feet, where it will stay until we arrive.

I know this.

I knew this that night.

So I fought tooth and nail to connect.

Step one of connection through feelings? It's to *notice how we feel*.

I asked myself a simple question: *How am I feeling?*

And here is what I said to myself in response: "I feel . . . not okay."

Now, we're going to spend the entirety of the next chapter talking about how to properly and precisely name our emotions, but as a baby step toward developing that competency, let's just start with two basic categories of feelings:

Okay.

And *Not Okay.*

Even with minimal training, we generally know when we're Okay, and we know *for sure* when we're Not Okay. Fair enough?

I was feeling Not Okay.

Great. A starting point. *I'm feeling Not Okay.*

I was astute enough in that moment to also detect that I was sad with a hint of despair. This combination was producing a lot of anxiety in me, which is why I was getting that itchy sensation I described.

I was experiencing some feelings, and I decided to *notice* that I was experiencing some feelings. This was real progress for me.

THE COST OF NOT NOTICING

For months on end, I've been thinking about this five-stage progression for engaging our emotions, and here's what I've noticed about noticing: We tend to notice a lot of things that don't matter much in the long run and not notice the things that do.

We notice when some celebrity has a new love interest. Or when our grocery store starts stocking our favorite chips. Or the annoying scuff mark on our favorite shoes that no amount of buffing can remove. Or the weird look on someone's face when we asked them for a favor.

On a given day, we notice a million things. We observe them; we take them in. We attend to them like we're into forensics, like our livelihood depends on our power to perceive.

Equally true: I could come up to you at any point on that same day and ask, "Hey, how are you feeling . . . for real?" And if you're like me and most people, there's so much going on inside that you don't even know how to respond. Even if we wanted to answer honestly (and that's a big *if,* given our control-cope-conceal tendencies), a response feels tricky to pin down.

So we all give the same reflexive answer.

Fine.

Fine!

Totally, completely fine.

When my kids were little and people used to ask me that question, and even now sometimes, life was so busy and so noisy that sometimes I just genuinely didn't know the answer. I want to give you compassion if that is true for you. Part of this process is slowing down enough to listen to our hearts, to listen to the parts of us that God built that we usually dismiss or judge. It's okay if you don't know how you're really feeling. Please do not beat yourself up for one minute in this whole process. It's also okay if you are feeling a hundred things all at once. It's okay.

If I could grab you by the face and ask you to do one thing for me in your journey toward emotional health, it is to resist the urge to judge yourself and these parts of you that might be waking up or screaming and going wild.

Now I want to ask you, how are you feeling right now? I mean *really* feeling?

My hope is that you would look at me and answer honestly either "Okay" or "Not Okay."

There is more to your present emotional state than this oversimplified response—of course there is. But it's a start. "Okay" and "Not Okay" are so, so, so much better than our preconditioned "Fine, fine—*really,* I'm fine! Totally and completely fine."

Suppressing your emotions can have lasting consequences. If you separate what you are experiencing inside from the people around you, it can make people perceive you as uninterested or inauthentic, and the energy required to suppress emotion can make it difficult to be present with other people.[1]

I know you think ignoring these emotions is not costing you anything. But it is.

According to a study by the Harvard School of Public Health and the University of Rochester, "People who bottled up their emotions even increased their chance of premature death from all causes by more than 30%, with their risk of being diagnosed with cancer increasing by 70%."[2]

We were built to feel.

Let me share some of my favorite science I found as I researched.[3] I think I loved it so much because it helps a little to untangle exactly how God built our emotions to work.

Emotions always enter in a three-phase approach:

1. *Inciting event:* You encounter an event as trivial as picking up your dry cleaning or as devastating as receiving a cancer diagnosis.

2. *Prediction:* Your mind (usually subconsciously) makes a prediction as to whether this is a positive or negative event.

3. *Effect:* Your body and mind react, and you manifest an emotional response.

If you possess the emotional, mental, and physical reserves to manage this new information, the event barely rocks the boat.

You feel it—no doubt about it—but you're able to respond in a healthy way.

But if you do *not* have the reserves to manage this news, your body and mind start to twitch and shut down.

Have you ever felt your heart race or chest tighten up and you don't even know why?

Recently, I was driving in the late afternoon. I had just picked up my dry cleaning and was making plans about what to cook for dinner. But I felt uneasy. My breath was short, and my chest felt tight. As I was trying to plan dinner, my mind kept racing—not to anything specific, just bouncing around like a ball. I was clearly having symptoms of anxiety, though I couldn't identify anything specific I was anxious about.

In that moment, I did a little assessment, which didn't produce much. I didn't have any glaring stress in this day. I had started out pretty content and had gotten a lot done. I couldn't remember any conflict I had experienced earlier in the day.

While nothing of importance was wrong, that day happened to fall inside a season of intense stress for me. Zac was spinning emotionally, our future and finances were less certain, and figuring out dinner and running a credit card for my dry cleaning were not the humdrum routines they once had been. Heading home meant debriefing with my husband about what difficult things had unfolded in his day and wondering what emotional state he would be in.

So, it was nothing: dry cleaners, dinner plans, ten-minute drive home. But it was also something because my reserves were running low. Scary low, in fact.

Listen, I am the queen of compartmentalization. I mean, how are we supposed to get anything done if the difficult things swirling in our lives are top of mind all the time? I'm great at stuffing my pain into a box on the shelf, a skill that often serves us well in seasons of stress.

But instead of staying quietly locked away, the pain increasingly demands attention—evidently, while I'm mindlessly tackling a dry-cleaning run.

So, let's imagine I refuse to dig a little deeper and neglect to figure out where that uneasy feeling is coming from. Let's say I try to keep it on the shelf and just figure out dinner.

Playing out this little scenario, I head home with my chest tight and my heart rate elevated (over a hundred, which I know because of my beloved Apple Watch) and my reserves dangerously low. I walk in and the house is a wreck and my children all need me and Zac has removed himself to our upstairs bedroom because he's feeling blue and his own reserves are depleted. And guess what I do? I *snap*. I lose it right there in front of my kids, who likely also had a stressful day, given their current challenges with dyslexia and bullies and expectations about how life should go. Their reserves are also very low. Sigh.

So, either I do all that (have a meltdown), or else . . . I notice what I'm feeling.

I notice what I'm feeling and why.

In *this* scenario, I walk into my house, I recognize the reality of my stressed family (some members of which are probably snapping at me), and instead of snapping back, I say, "Hey, how about we sit down and talk about our day? I had a rough one. I have been worried about some things with Dad, and I almost just lost it in the car."

And then one kid says, "Ugh. Me too. Someone was making fun of me, and I'm so tired of getting picked on."

And another kid says, "I had a bad day too. I got a C on a test I thought I did okay on."

And my husband comes down and we hug, and instead of pretending everything is fine, he tells the kids what was hard about his day, and we sit down for our thrown-together dinner and eat it right there *in* our hard. We face the hard together. And it's messy, and it's right, and the hard gets lighter as we carry it together.

Emotions are best healed in community. They are best healed there because they were given to us to connect us to others. Crying alone is cathartic; crying together heals us.

Inciting events are happening everywhere. Your mind and body have predicted their cost, and it's high. And yes, you are being affected by every last event.

Also true: Given all that's going on around us, your reserves are probably lower than they've ever been. And God and I (and I hope someone else in your life) can look at you and say, "Of *course* you feel this way. Because it's all so hard."

NOTICING IS ESSENTIAL TO CONNECTING

In Mark 5, we meet a woman who has been bleeding for twelve years and desperately wants to be healed. There's a crowd around Jesus when she sees Him, and she pushes through and touches His garment and is instantly healed. But Jesus is a noticer, and He stops everything. And He looks for her and asks who just touched Him. And the woman comes to Jesus, and she is trembling with fear.

I imagine Jesus cradling her face in His hands, looking her in the eyes, and declaring His delight over her. "Daughter, your faith has made you well; go in peace, and be healed of your disease."[4] See, it wasn't enough for Jesus to heal her; He wanted a relationship with her. He stopped in the midst of a crowd and noticed a woman who had been ostracized all her life. He didn't just want her to stop bleeding; He wanted to look her in the eyes and connect with her and begin a relationship with her. Using intimate language: "Daughter."

The woman had to notice what she needed and believe that Jesus could heal her. The woman had to be brave enough to push through every barrier to touch Him and be close to Him. The second she did, Jesus turned and found her, healing not only her body but initiating a relationship with Him that would go on forever.

Listen, I know this process might feel intimidating or scary, especially if you grew up in a home where feelings were barely recognized. Or maybe you just feel so much that you're scared your emotions might overtake you if you stop to notice the grief you've been pushing away. I know this isn't easy.

The truth about you and me is that we spend so much time in our thoughts—in our head—that it may feel awkward to *feel* for once. My advice is to persevere. Give this thing a try. Notice the feelings you're feeling. Acknowledge that they are there.

I know firsthand how tempting it is to deny that what you're feeling is what you're feeling, but **we do ourselves no favors when we fake that we're okay.** Psychology confirms that emotions are intricately connected to our motivational system, which means we need to feel our feelings if we hope to get anything done.[5] If we want to exist in a meaningful relationship, we have to feel our feelings. If we want to forgo temptation, we have to feel our feelings. If we want to experience pleasure, we have to feel our feelings. If we want to move through pain, it's those feelings we simply must feel.

So, here's what I want you to do once you put down this book and go on with your day: The next time you feel a feeling rise in yourself—in your body, in your brain, in your spirit, in your soul—I want you to stop what you're doing. Just for a second, you can stop. Notice the feeling instead of brushing it aside. Connect with it.

If it's helpful, ask yourself these two questions:

1. *What do I sense in myself emotionally? Am I Okay or Not Okay?*

2. *Can I sit with either reality for a bit?*

You can take things one step further by asking a third question, which is this:

3. *How long have I been feeling this way? For an hour? A day? A year? Since age ten?*

We'll build on this progress in the chapters to come, but for now, noticing is enough. If you're having trouble determining whether you're Okay or Not Okay, tune in to your body for a minute and see if you find any clues. **Our bodies are constantly feeding us information about how we're doing, but we have to pay attention to learn.**

Recently, a friend stopped by my place to talk with me about one of her struggles. After she got settled, I asked, "Where do you feel your feelings in your body right now?"

"In my shoulders," she said. "I can't get them to relax from my ears."

Telling, right?

Maybe for you it is bouncing knees, an inability to sit still, tightness in your chest, or nausea.

Take a minute and notice your body. Where do you feel different emotions?

Find a seat in a quiet space.

Close your eyes.

Put your feet on the ground.

Start at your feet and notice your body.

Is there any pain?

Is there any discomfort?

Do you have a headache?

Is your jaw tight?

Are your shoulders slumped?

Is your chest tight?

Is your stomach upset? Do you feel butterflies in it?

Are your hands shaking?

What did you notice?

We're so accustomed to blowing off our bodies' signals that it's always astounding when we first realize how chatty they have been all along.

THE BEGINNING OF A WHOLEHEARTED LIFE

Let me give you a couple of examples of how powerful noticing can be. The first involves one of my kids, and for that person's protection—and in case this person isn't all that interested in being outed here in Mom's book—I'll refer to this person as Kid.

Kid has always struggled with feeling feelings. For years, really the only emotion Kid expressed was anger. You and I both know that anger is often a disguise for other emotions (sadness, frustration, fear), but what always came out was anger, just pure, unvarnished rage.

After trying all sorts of interventions, Zac and I decided that Kid might benefit from going to see a counselor. We booked a few appointments and watched for signs of life.

A session went by, and nothing changed. Two sessions: still no change. But after about three sessions of high-quality therapy, Kid started to notice (key word!) that other emotions were there. They'd been there all along, of course, even as Kid had refused to take note.

You'll appreciate this: The same night that I was experiencing that wave of anxiety due to my feeling sad, with a hint of despair, Kid was having an all-out meltdown on the patio, sobbing, head buried in hands. I remember pulling up momentarily from my own downward spiral to whisper, "Wait. What? Is my kid feeling *sad*? Yes. Win!" Who is happy their kid feels sad? Anyone who sees these emotions as gifts. Because we all need to feel sad sometimes. And this was the first time something other than anger had emerged from them. It was a win!

To be sure, Kid still has a lot of work to do before I would describe this person as emotionally healthy, resilient, or mature. But in them admitting that other feelings are present—noticing them, finally—we are making progress.

Here's another example: I was talking with a teammate recently about some of these ideas, and she said, "If I give you a real-world scenario, will you coach me through it?"

After I said yes, she explained that though she is well into the middle of her life, she *still* struggles with a debilitating perfectionism that keeps her from enjoying even obvious wins. She'd had one such win a few days before we talked and was annoyed that she couldn't relish it. "What gives?" she asked.

I used the same questions with her that I'm asking you to practice asking yourself. First up: "Well, how would you say you're doing? Not Okay, I presume."

"Not Okay," she confirmed. "I feel like I can't measure up."

We talked a little about that, and then I said, "Think back. When did you first feel the feeling that you're feeling right now?"

I'm not exaggerating even a little bit when I tell you that, without missing a beat, the woman pinpointed for me time, place, and exactly what she was wearing when it happened. She was a child! Just ten years old. Standing in the kitchen with her mom and dad. Excitedly telling her parents about school that day. Wearing a white cap-sleeve T-shirt with a giant rainbow on the chest, jean shorts, and cherry-red Keds.

"My dad had just gotten home from work, and I ran into the kitchen to tell him how great I did on my math test that day, but then everything fell apart."

She went on to tell me that after she'd asked her dad to guess what she'd gotten on her test, he'd guessed one hundred—a perfect score. In fact, she'd gotten a ninety-eight, and while it was absolutely a grade to be proud of, somehow she internalized the message that day that a ninety-eight wasn't perfect enough.

We talked about how common it is to make greater meaning out of the things we hear from the powerful people in our young lives than what those people may have meant and about how challenging it is to rewind to those early memories and unwind those threads from our hearts.

It *is* tough.

Also, it is worth it.

In this chapter and the next few, I've included stories from five friends of mine who have gone on similar journeys of untangling their emotions and who personally confirm that the freedom they've found is absolutely worth every bit of the hard work they've invested.

I encouraged my teammate to start her journey of healing by noticing those feelings of inadequacy and recognizing that they've been around awhile. That's as far as you and I have gotten to-

Emotional Awareness: A Personal Story

Have you ever reacted to one of your kids in a way that far exceeded what they actually did? I had begun to notice a pattern of overreaction toward one of my kids in particular, when a friend told me, "The number one thing you can do for your kids is to make sense of your own story."

So I started to simply pay attention to my feelings in these moments and ask myself, *"What do I feel?"* And then, *"When did I first feel that in my life?"* Nine times out of ten, a moment or story from my own life as a child emerged that needed to be named. As I began to name and share my own story on a regular basis with others in my community and as that story was received with love, the part of me that reacted became more quiet. More still. I began to experience what Psalm 131:2 calls a quieted soul: "I have

gether, and although more is to come on how to heal from those wounds, *noticing* is sufficient for now.

But I will also say this: If that colleague follows the rest of the progression that you and I will talk about in chapters to come, then she will learn how to befriend that younger version of herself and help that younger her heal.

And the same is true for you.

A quick aside before we move on: My friend told me that when she looks back on that younger version of herself, she feels pity toward her, almost like she's ashamed of that little girl for letting

calmed and quieted my soul, like a weaned child with its mother; like a weaned child is my soul within me."

I soon learned that emotional awareness creates choice and that choices are empowering! Instead of reacting, I could eventually learn to pause, feel my feelings, and then respond. It sounds so simple, yet to this day, it still requires so much effort to tune in to myself. But this kind of tuning in and allowing parts of me to receive love and acceptance from others is fueling me to parent my kids in a more wholehearted (and holy) way.

Though I've finally accepted that no formula exists for perfect parenting that results in perfect kids, this approach is helping me to better recognize both my needs and theirs.

—Jessica, age forty-six

someone else rob her of happiness, for letting her dad's comment hold such sway over her heart.

When I heard that assessment, I wanted to cry. "Wow," I said. "I can tell you wish you'd handled things differently back then, but honestly, what was ten-year-old you to do? Our parents are such influential people in our lives when we're growing up! I have a totally different take on things."

When I thought about the ten-year-old version of this friend, who to me always seems strong and sure, I felt deep compassion for her. I wanted to pull that child into a tight embrace, wrapping her up in my arms, delighting over her with smiles and laughter. I wanted to throw that little girl a huge party and celebrate her awesome test score. I wanted to put my hands on her cheeks, look directly into her eyes, and tell her she should be *so* very proud of herself. I wanted to help her see that she'd won, not lost—that she was not just not inadequate but also amazing in my eyes.

The best news of all? Knowing what I know of this process we're embarking on, I won't be surprised even a little bit when she comes to me at some point a month or year from now and says, "Hey, I'm starting to kind of like the ten-year-old me."

And it all will have started with *noticing*: paying attention to what we're sensing in our feelings, acknowledging that those feelings are true for us, and remembering when the emotions we're experiencing first showed themselves in our lives.

AS WE MOVE together through the progression of connection with our emotions, it might be wise to slow down and sit with each chapter for a few days. Practice each step. Lean into this. It might feel clumsy at first. As you practice each phase of the progression, it will become innate and more natural.

Above all, I encourage you to invite God into this journey with you.

If you are scared of feeling these feelings, ask Him for strength to face them.

If you are confused about what you are feeling, ask Him for insight and clarity.

If you are overwhelmed with feelings, ask Him to issue peace that surpasses understanding.

If you are numb and don't feel anything, ask Him to wake up your heart.

He loves you. He made you. He made these emotions so that you would draw near to Him. This is how we do that. Talk to Him about it all.

9

THE VOCABULARY
OF EMOTION

NOTICE

NAME

FEEL

SHARE

CHOOSE

"How does that make you feel?"

It is my very least favorite question my counselor asks, and he asks it all the time. In the beginning of our time together, I hated it so much because I honestly just didn't know. I didn't know how I felt. I couldn't quite place it. And that scared me. So, I guess when he asked me how I felt . . . I felt scared.

Scared that I couldn't locate my heart and therefore scared that the answer he seemed to think should be obvious—and maybe it was to everyone but me—was not.

Yet here we were again, and again I didn't know how I felt. I couldn't name it.

I have a friend who likes to quote the apostle Paul, saying, "I am 'hard pressed on every side,'"[1] and then adds, "but there is one small side that is okay." So I'm fine. I'm fine. I have this one little side that is just fine.

At times, we are asked, "How are you really feeling?" and we say, "Fine," and we mean it. Other times, we say, "Fine," because it is the only option. Everyone needs us, and what else are we supposed to do? If we fall apart and let all our feelings out, our world might implode.

And that's okay. Sometimes controlling, coping, and concealing can help us get through the seasons when the absolutely best we can do is just survive.

But eventually all those evasive tactics become ingrained. It's simply our normal way of life. And we become a bit of a programmed robot. Not just in the way we answer the question of how we are, but also in the way we become detached from our own feelings.

Counseling taught me that I had forgotten how to feel. I had forgotten how to notice what I feel and name it. So I didn't feel anymore. Until I learned how to feel again. I had to learn how to notice and name what I feel, like a kindergartner with a feelings chart pointing to a smiley face or an angry face or a sad little stick-figure face with a tear coming down its cheek.

I had to learn to feel again, and it all started with noticing everything happening on the insides of me and learning once again to name it.

Maybe you feel like that kindergartner who can't even decide what face to point to on an emoji chart. That's okay.

I got you. We are going to dig into this.

NAMING IMPLIES AUTHORITY

Humans have a deep-seated need to name stuff. We name our children. We name our vehicles. We nickname our friends. We put words to our resolutions and our years. We ascribe this sort of meaning to just about everything, as a way to identify it, as a way to set it apart, as a way to honor it, as a way to keep it organized.

We use words to make better sense of things. We use words to bring order to our worlds.

From the beginning of time, naming has been synonymous with authority. God names Adam and Eve and then gives them dominion over the animals and earth, and they name the animals.

I like the imagery of naming to tame because it applies so perfectly to our emotions. Think about it: Why would you want to tame something unless it's to bring it a little closer to you?

We tame, or "break," horses so that we can ride them.

We tame certain breeds of cats and dogs so that they can peacefully live in our homes.

We tame rowdy kids so that we can stay sane as we go through life.

"If you want to tame it, name it," Dr. Daniel Siegel once famously said.[2]

My point: To tame something is to remind that thing that it is not in control. Now, I am quick to point out that *we* are not in control either. What we're aiming for, as it relates to emotions, is the sort of relationship that characterizes a two-person dance.

We want to work with our emotions, not against them.

Why is this so hard?

Many of us weren't taught how to identify our feelings. Or we were discouraged from giving voice to them.

Many of us worry that if we are sad or angry, it might be a sin.

Some of us even learned that if we feel happy, we probably are wrong.

We're so busy and distracted that it's easier not to think about the hard.

We don't think anything can change, so we don't see the point.

It feels trivial to feel negative emotions when our lives aren't so bad.

We're scared that if we stop controlling, coping, and concealing, our feelings will take over our lives.

But honestly naming what we are feeling is essential to untangling our insides. Jesus constantly asked people questions to get them to name what was true about the deepest parts of their souls.

What do you want?

Why are you so afraid?

Why did you doubt?

What do you want Me to do for you?

Do you love Me?[3]

He usually began with a diagnosis, but He didn't give it to people; He sent them to discover it for themselves. Unless they wouldn't—and then in love, He would state the truth for them. For example, He met the woman at the well exactly where she was in her despair and embarrassment and hiding, and when He gave her the chance to say what was true and she withheld, He told her everything she was ashamed of. He named it for her when she wasn't brave enough to name it herself.

And He met her with relationship, hope, and promise—not the shame and guilt she was accustomed to feeling. He surprised her with His love for her, and they never could have connected unless the fear and guilt she felt were named.

YOU FEEL—YOU AREN'T YOUR FEELINGS

Emotional maturity is the ability to feel what we feel without judgment and without being controlled by our emotions. Emotional wholeness begins by noticing and naming what we feel and then deciding what to do with it, allowing these emotions to draw us to God and one another.

We're talking about healing. We're talking about wholeheartedness. We're talking about feeling deeply and connecting deeply with God and others because of it. **But too many of us don't have a vocabulary to describe our feelings, or we've misunderstood what constitutes an emotion.**

For example, I fear we've raised a generation to believe that anxiety and depression are feelings. They're not. They're pathologies. Something the doctor diagnoses.

I hope I've shared enough of my family's story for you to know we get mental illness around here. We get depression that can't be shaken off. We get anxiety that requires medicine and counseling. Praise God for the help those things have been in our lives. But clinical anxiety and depression are not our feelings.

Feelings are grief and worry and anguish. And hope and contentment and joy. Because we've never learned to name and share and feel these feelings, we end up with pathologies. Yes, sometimes it's just the brokenness of our fallen world. Our bodies don't make the right chemicals and there's nothing we can do about it except treat it as a medical condition.

But even with a diagnosis, if we want to make progress toward health, we have to learn to feel the spectrum of all the feelings. Any doctor or counselor will tell you it's not enough to take medicine. It's not enough to treat the chemical problem. You have to learn to name the pain, share the pain, and heal from the pain. That can take a long time because we spent decades learning how to control, cope, or conceal. Changing that can take more than a minute. We can't help what we didn't learn. We can only fight to learn it and do it differently for ourselves and for the next generation.

People can change. People do change.

I watched it right in front of me when Zac learned to feel. He learned it, and it made him into the most present and compassionate husband, friend, father, and even God follower. He learned to feel.

We are going to put words to our feelings. Let's go.

THE BIG FOUR

As you begin to think about how to name the feelings you're feeling, I want to offer you four places to start.

In chapter 8, the noticing phase, we simply assessed whether we were Okay or Not Okay. Pretty basic, I know. Now we are working to deepen that articulation by *categorizing* our level of Okayness or Not Okayness with better, richer words.

I want to touch briefly on the Big Four when it comes to emotions, with a huge caveat that depending on which emotions expert you consult, you'll get a very different head count:

There are four main emotions.

No, there are five!

Wrong. There are seven.

Nope. There are twenty-one!

I've opted for four, because my brain can remember four.[4] However, as your emotional intelligence grows, the goal is increased specificity—to be able to name with greater detail what you are really feeling. So, under all four primary emotions, I have listed several secondary emotions by order of increasing intensity. This matters because if a friend asks you how you feel and you say, "I feel sad," that *sadness* could be more specifically *disappointment* that you were left out of a get-together. Or it could be *despair* because your father was just diagnosed with terminal cancer. Your friend's response will, naturally, be tempered to the specifics, and the response in your own heart and body will be distinctly different depending on the particulars and intensity of the emotion.

No one has to teach you how to feel. A baby comes out and feels sad and happy and needy and wanting. These feelings are innate, universal. And they tell a watching world what we need and what we want and what we are thinking, even before we have the words to say it. We come out of the comfort of the womb into a bright unknown world, and we feel sad, angry, maybe even delighted. Those emotions actually help us survive because our expression of those feelings prompts those around us to connect and respond.

And right from the start, we can feel a range of feelings at the same time. I didn't realize it was possible to have so many parts of ourselves until I went to counseling. Part of me can be afraid and part of me can be excited and part of me sad at the exact same time about the exact same event. Somehow I didn't know that. I just felt confused. For instance, you can be getting married and feel joy but also feel grief because your dad passed away five years ago and isn't there. You can be overwhelmed and nervous about your work and also find joy in it. You can feel annoyed with the toddler stage that your child is in and also be grateful and trying to savor it.

Understanding that part of you can experience one thing and another part of you can experience a wholly different thing at the same time is an element of what it means to be human. When God made us in His image, he gave us the capacity to carry many things all at once.

So, as we look at the Big Four, make an effort to notice and name where each one is present in your life right now or when it most often appears. Bonus points if you can find a more nuanced word to describe more specifically how it shows itself in each instance.

 JOY   SATISFIED AMUSEMENT PEACE COMFORT REJOICING DELIGHT **EXCITEMENT**

Let's start here! Because we all want joy, right? Happiness is an addiction in our culture; we crave it. Maybe you are a naturally joyful person. Or maybe it's been a while since you felt truly happy.

When was the last time you felt ecstatic, giddy, really happy?

Here is the thing about joy: You'll never notice or appreciate it unless you learn to feel sadness and fear and anger too.

I recently saw a scan of a brain all lit up with enjoyment. The next image showed the brain all lit up with fear. Although the emotions were identified with completely different colors, it was clear they were showing up in similar regions. **You can't turn off**

the parts of your brain that feel sadness and anger without also shutting down your ability to feel joy.

Some of us love these moments and drink them in, fully present. But maybe you are in a season of so much difficulty—the loss of a spouse or parents, or having an illness or wayward child—that you cannot remember the last time you felt joy, the last time you laughed. Again, I just wish we were doing this over coffee and I could grab your hands and cry with you or laugh with you.

Joy can be a complicated one. Sometimes we feel guilty if we aren't joyful, as if it is the absolute required state for people of faith, and then sometimes we feel guilty when we feel happy, for a myriad of reasons, not the smallest that the Enemy loves to steal, kill, and destroy joy.[5] At times I have been in a season of celebration that is difficult to enjoy because so many others are suffering. Being happy feels like a betrayal to them, you know?

That is why this process is so important. Basically, 99.9 percent of what we are feeling and all the ways those emotions are affecting us and those we love is involuntary and unnoticed. We never process that tinge of guilt we feel about being happy, so the two emotions gradually become so intertwined that guilt steals joy every time it presents itself to us.

But Christ came so that we would have life abundant in Him.[6] He delighted over children, over meals with friends, over people coming to faith, over people being healed, over wine at a wedding. He said to His disciples, "These things I have spoken to you, that my joy may be in you, and that your joy may be full."[7] Full of joy. Joy is a fruit of the Spirit, and it is a gift from God. We reflect His image when we feel joy.

What would change in your day if you were to start noticing the things that make you happy and adding them into your life?

IRRITATED FRUSTRATED BITTER HATRED OUTRAGE RAGE

The world is full of injustice. Abuse and neglect warrant our anger. God is angry with sin. We have a righteous anger within us that cries out against injustice, and there are specific times when we need to stand up in defense of biblical priorities. The Holy Spirit leads us in how to respond to injustice big and small as we lean into Him. There is a time and place for action and a time and place to pursue reconciliation.

God doesn't tell us to never get angry. Because He knows we are so easily offended, His call is that we be "slow to anger."[8] And in doing this, we live like God, whom the Bible describes as "a God merciful and gracious, slow to anger, and abounding in steadfast love and faithfulness."[9]

He also calls us to not sin in our anger,[10] and that is the dang hard part. We live in an outraged society where everybody is offended all the time. But that doesn't make anger evil. **It's what we do with our anger that determines if something good turns into something bad.**

God built our nervous system with a fight-or-flight reaction, so every human has a built-in capacity to react to their circumstances. Yet in our world, we've been trained from a young age that those reactions are dangerous and unhealthy.

When your adrenaline starts pumping and you want to cuss because a car pulls out in front of you, or when the chaos of getting your family out the door to go somewhere makes you want to poke your eyeballs out, or your heart races as you walk alone through a deserted parking garage, that's all because God built a system in your body to react to any danger or uncomfortable circumstance that you might face.

It's why judging our reactions is not really helpful. What is helpful is understanding and accepting that we will get angry. We will react to the world around us. But noticing and naming our anger is essential to choosing what we will do with it.

Let me give you an example:

You get mad.

You hate that feeling.

You don't know what to do with it.

You ignore it, but you can't.

Now what?

Well, if it's not a situation you can control, maybe you cope. You drink that anger away. Or you yell it away.

But instead you remember that God says, "In your anger do not sin."[11] Shoot. This makes our response to anger more complicated. What are we going to do with it?

Now, remember, our feelings are meant to lead us to connection with God and other people. And anger frequently rises up in us because we feel misunderstood. So often, it isn't a problem with another person; it's a problem within ourselves. We are misunderstood. We are lost. We are mad someone didn't get punished for something they did wrong to us or someone we love.

But imagine if we let our anger draw us to God instead of to sin, instead of to berating the person at the checkout line or those closest to us.

God, this feels unfair. Why are You not fixing this? You are able to fix it, and You're not. And I don't know what to do with this rage I feel. Will You help me and show me what You want me to know and what You want me to do?

And then you listen and you wait.

.   .   .

Three things just happened:

1. You meditated and slowed your breathing, which science tells us is the greatest thing you can do in a moment of rage.

2. You transferred authority over the situation from yourself to God.

3. You invited the Holy Spirit into an impossible situation to show you His power and gave Him room to work.

When was the last time you felt frustrated with someone? When was the last time you got flat mad?

 SAD   DISAPPOINTED   MELANCHOLY   LONELY   HELPLESS   HOPELESS   GRIEF   **ANGUISH**

Sadness is another one of those feelings that gets a bad rap. **Too many of us have bought into the idea that if we're not continuously exuding joy, then we're not representing our faith well.** But sadness is actually in the Bible a lot, where it's often called *lament,* and we see it expressed by all kinds of people in the context of faithfully pursuing God's heart. The prophets lament, God's people lament, even Jesus laments in the Garden of Gethsemane, as we will see. And psalm after psalm in the middle of your Bible is full of lament.

But we're afraid of it? I think of my friend from India who lost her mother and felt confused that Americans simply dropped a casserole off and hoped she would feel better soon. We are anti-lament. And it costs us.[12]

You want to know why everyone's cranky and in a bad mood and annoyed by everything?

Because we don't know how to lament. Rather than grieving the difficult things that are happening all around us on a given day, we pass by them and try not to give them too much attention. That might be wise concerning the barrage of news stories that could otherwise engulf us. But it is unwise when we push down the reality of pain in our own lives that's inescapable and unavoidable.

Let me take some of the pressure off: There's not a right way to be sad—you're just sad. There's not a right way to go through trauma—it just is horrible.

As I've noted before, I love David in all his messy, wild emotions. The guy dances naked in the streets to praise God and wears sackcloth and ashes to repent. Today we would call him an emotional train wreck, but God called him "a man after his own heart."[13] He lamented a lot. He felt safe to do it because of what he wrote in Psalm 103:13–14: "As a father shows compassion to his children, so the LORD shows compassion to those who fear him. For he knows our frame; he remembers that we are dust." It's a picture of a father with his kid, gracious that they're a mess, compassionate that they're very upset about it, and glad they came to him with it all.

When was the last time you cried? When was the last time you pushed away sadness? What triggers your sadness most often?

UNREST DOUBT NERVOUS WORRY DREAD PANIC TERROR

Fear is on a mission to keep us safe. Sometimes it tells us there is imminent danger, and sometimes it scares us about an unknown future, robbing us of sleep. We so quickly demonize it. I think of how long I misunderstood all the "Fear not" language throughout the Bible. I've heard a hundred sermons telling us how much God does not want us to fear, as if it were a command instead of an invitation.

I'm going to set a lot of those passages right here, and I want you to read them differently. I want you to picture a loving, safe father speaking to his child who is freaking out, crying, and afraid:

- "Fear not, for I am with you; be not dismayed, for I am your God; I will strengthen you, I will help you, I will uphold you with my righteous right hand."

- "Do not be afraid of them, for I am with you to deliver you."

- "Take heart; it is I. Do not be afraid."

- "Don't be afraid; you are worth more than many sparrows."

- "Fear not, little flock, for it is your Father's good pleasure to give you the kingdom."

- "Peace I leave with you; my peace I give you. I do not give to you as the world gives. Do not let your hearts be troubled and do not be afraid."[14]

In each of these instances, something scary was impending and God was essentially saying, "Eyes on Me." His command was meant to issue comfort. Knowing the facts often alleviates our fear. God wants us to know that we don't have to be afraid. He is with us, and He is for us.

But He's not scolding us like a disappointed father when we fear. Otherwise, we would be afraid of being afraid. No, He is comforting us with truth. **Fear is our constant reminder we need God and that He is there.** He is with us in the valleys.

Like every emotion, fear can entangle you and become a stronghold, but it is more likely to do that if you do not recognize it, name it, and share it with others.

Steps Toward Freedom: A Personal Story

As a pastor, I had taught on anxiety countless times. Then I actually experienced it.

Looking back, I realize I was only teaching about worry before. Anxiety was different. Bigger. Scarier. I didn't think I could get through it. It felt like it jumped on me and was pulling me down into the pit of depression. It felt like my capacity was cut in half or fourths and I wouldn't be able to crawl out of this dark place. It even affected how my heart would beat.

My cardiologist referred me to a therapist. My community rallied around me in prayer. I began to meditate, and in taking small steps of obedience, I began to see the light at the end of the tunnel.

I have found a deeper, more meaningful relationship with Jesus and a joy rooted in the kindness of God.

—Jonathan, age forty-two

.   .   .

When was the last time you remember feeling worried or afraid? How can you imagine God viewing you in that moment?

LET'S GIVE IT A TRY

Let me introduce you to a concept you've likely not heard before: *emotional granularity*.[15] Isn't that a cool term?

Emotional granularity is the ability to describe your emotional state using nuanced words and phrases instead of generic ones.

Here's what's fascinating about emotional granularity: Feelings experts have shown that there is a direct proportional connection between a person's emotional granularity and their mental health, physical health, and relational health. "The more specifically you are able to describe what is going on inside you, the more flexible you will become in the face of that emotion. Growing in specificity has even been linked with fewer doctor appointments and medications and better social and emotional functioning."[16]

That's interesting, isn't it?

What this means is that as you and I expand our vocabulary to express our feelings, our health in three key aspects of life will also start to expand. Those extra words listed in this chapter beside each of the Big Four can serve as helpful reference points as you begin to practice naming.

Ready to play?

Here we go.

What is the biggest challenge you are facing right now, and what emotions are attached to it?

.   .   .

Maybe you and your spouse are struggling in your marriage, and hopelessness is rising for you.

Maybe money is tighter than ever and despair is taking hold.

It could be that you've wanted to have a baby for years now but still there's an empty crib. Frustration over feeling abandoned by God, jealousy over friends' pregnancy announcements, embarrassment over a body that seems to have failed you—what emotion aren't you feeling?

We need words to make better sense of things.

With more words, things make far more sense.

But it's going to take some practice to make naming our feelings a stronger habit than evading them. So, as you seek to engage more authentically with the real ways that you're feeling, just start here: Throughout your day today, I want you to pause periodically and tell yourself how you feel.

Right now, how do you feel? Look through the emotions listed on the preceding pages and pick the most specific word you can.

If you don't like talking to yourself out loud, then you're welcome to just think the thought. But I want you to actually think or say a complete sentence about how you feel at different points throughout the day. Set a reminder on your phone if you need to.

You might say to yourself, "I feel *hopeful* in this relationship." Or maybe, "I feel *encouraged* with my progress so far." Or, "I feel *excited* about this assignment." Or, "I'm not angry; I just feel *curious.*"

Maybe you feel somber. Or joyful. Or grateful for something simple in your day. Maybe you feel irritated. Or exasperated. Or feisty. Or ecstatic. Or calm.

Fight to go beyond telling yourself something benign, such as, "I feel fine." "I feel okay." "I'm good."

THE WAY IT'S MEANT TO WORK

Last night my son-in-law, Charlie, was over, along with my daughter Kate. As we were talking about this book, he showed me the app he uses multiple times every day, How We Feel. Three times a day, he and Kate and many of their friends enter in how they feel.

The first field to complete is generally equivalent to "Are you okay?" Then it leads you to name the actual specific emotion you relate to most. Then—are you ready for this?—it shares your answer with your closest people who are also on the app.

They told us that recently the app alerted my daughter that one of her friends was feeling panicked! Kate immediately called her friend: "Are you okay?" The friend started crying and told Kate what difficult thing she was in the middle of.

Then the friend asked, "How did you know?"

She'd forgotten about the alert feature. But as we will talk about later, that silly app worked just like it was meant to, drawing people closer to the real parts of us. That closeness is what we are craving.

And it's what we miss if we never name what is really going on.

10

GIVE YOURSELF SOME SPACE

NOTICE

NAME

FEEL

SHARE

CHOOSE

In a book about feeling our feelings, you could say that this chapter is the most important of all. We have noticed our feelings. We have named our feelings. And now, at last, we feel them.

It may strike you as funny that we have to include this step—ready, set, *feel*!—but if you're a recovering fixer like I am, then you'll quickly realize the benefits of being forced to feel instead.

Before we jump in, though, I want to issue a warning. Well, it's not a warning, exactly. It's more of a *consideration*. It's possible that you will get to this stage in our process of connecting through our emotions and realize you're just not ready to feel the feelings you feel. Yeah, you've noticed them. You've even named them. But maybe, for a whole host of reasons, it will not serve you well to feel.

You could be on a deadline for a work project and simply don't have capacity to deal with them.

You could be recovering from trauma and are concerned that a deep dive into your true feelings will set you back instead of move you ahead.

You could be facing a new set of unforeseen and undesirable circumstances, and feeling for real might vaporize the last bit of energy you possess.

Whatever the reason, there will be times when doing the earnest work of feeling just isn't the right step for you to take. We all have seasons like these, and my advice whenever you encounter one is to simply let the feeling drift by.

When Zac spiraled into his first real emotional low back in 2014, I pictured myself standing on the shore watching waves of feelings crash at my feet. I noticed them. I could have named them if you'd asked me to. But I couldn't jump into those waves and really experience what I was feeling, for fear that I'd be utterly swept away. I was in survival mode—not just for myself, but on behalf of my family. I'd have to deal with those emotions someday. But someday wasn't *that* day.

You may have to do the same thing.

If you find yourself in survival mode for any reason at all, go ahead and stay firmly planted on the shoreline. You can watch those waves coming in, one after another after another. Notice them. Acknowledge and name them for what they are. Just know that you don't have to experience them until you're ready. My guess is that you'll intuitively know when it's time.

ONCE YOU'RE READY TO FEEL

With my caveat out of the way, let's talk about how to feel. I am going to walk you through a simple approach to feeling a feeling. This may seem strange. *To feel a feeling, don't you just, you know . . . feel?*

Yeah, yeah, yeah. Show-off.

For some people, it's not that easy. Think of it this way: Most of us know in our heads the difference between hot and cold, but to sit and feel, absorb, enjoy the warmth of a summer day is entirely different than just noting and naming that it's sunny outside. If it is raining, you can notice, or you can go outside and let it soak into your skin.

This is our attempt to feel the rain on our faces.

Take your time. Read slowly through the following parts and give yourself space. This is not exactly something you can rush.

PART 1: PAUSE

This might be the most difficult thing I ask you to do. Right here. Right now.

In my most difficult seasons of life, to stop and pay attention meant the possibility of drowning in it all. It's possible you are in a season where the feeling you need to let in is that of happiness and joy, but more likely the pause I am asking you to take might mean that, after a mere minute, tears begin to fall that have needed to fall for a long time. Sometimes all it takes is a quiet minute free of all our typical distractions to feel everything we need to feel.

The quiet can feel like an unwelcome friend. The tears or anger or facing the fear you have been afraid to feel certainly can feel unwelcome as well.

I'm sorry. I wish I were there with you. I imagine you right now held by God in the quiet pause with whatever comes.

PART 2: GIVE YOURSELF PERMISSION

I think back to the car ride after my great-grandmother's funeral. I never gave my parents a chance to comfort me. I never gave myself the freedom to cry loud enough for them to even hear me. I was so ashamed of feeling sad.

But if I could go back and see that little seven-year-old crying in the back seat, I would wrap her up and rock her and say, "Yes! Of course you are crying at death! Of course you are confused and don't know what to make of it all. The adults don't either." I would hold her and make her feel safe to cry at the darkness and confusion in the world.

Ah, if only we could go back.

But remember? We actually can.

That's what we're doing here. We're healing parts of us that have never healed.

So, after pausing and sinking into the feeling you're feeling, give yourself permission to feel it to its fullest.

Just feel what you're feeling.

Accept the feeling, exactly as it is.

And that part of you that is judging you and saying why you shouldn't feel that way—just quiet that part of you and feel anyway.

PART 3: LOOK BACK

Pause. Give permission. And now this: *Look back.*

I want you to look back at the feelings we named in the previous chapter and think of a *recent* time when you felt a strong reaction, a time when one of those feelings was clear to you. What was the feeling you felt? When was the first time you remember feeling that feeling? Maybe you were six years old, or maybe you were twenty.

For example, not long ago, my sister Katie called me from an airport. Her heart was racing, and she felt a sense of dread. When we surveyed together what could be causing those things, we decided that most of her life seemed in order and there wasn't a really good reason.

However, two terrible dramatic moments from years ago came to mind, two times in her life she has had to shoulder unthinkable news, the kind of news we can't write in books because it's just too hard. And guess where she was both times she got that kind of news? Alone in an airport.

So, yes, even though nothing traumatic was happening last week in that airport, her body and mind still carry those events, and, of course, being alone in an airport brings back fear.

We stayed on the phone together and talked about how crazy it is that feelings can flood us without any warning just because our body is in a specific location. My sister felt the waves and walked through them with me on the phone.

Katie has been in counseling for long enough to know that the fear wasn't actually going to take her down. She could see clearly that the fear was just a remnant of a reality that truly, deeply used to be hers. She's been given tools to change and grow. So, upon peeking back and seeing that the she she once was is not the she she is today, she was able to say to her fear with all sincerity, *Oh, right, it's you again. Well, come on, then. It's time to go.*

Better than just about anyone I know, my little sister lives out the passage that says, "Count it all joy, my brothers, when you meet trials of various kinds, for you know that the testing of your faith produces steadfastness. And let steadfastness have its full effect, that you may be perfect and complete, lacking in nothing."[1]

Katie wasn't taken down by her feelings. She felt them, she reached out to me, and, with the perspective of her past, she could take those feelings along as she did what she needed to do and boarded her flight.

PART 4: PERSIST

What Katie was doing was accepting the feeling and its ramifications, without reservation and without legislation regarding how that feeling should behave, which is part four: *Persist with the feeling* instead of fighting against it. Let it be what it already is.

I know. That goes against every inclination prompted by our lifelong habit of emotional evasion. But although our patterns of controlling, coping, and concealing are often rooted in a desire to reduce stress, according to researcher and addiction expert Dr. Gabor Maté, "the healthy expression of emotion is itself stress-reducing."[2]

In other words, **if we would just express our authentic emo-**

tions instead of looking for a way out of that expression, we could potentially bypass the stress response altogether and just get on with our lives.

In a *Psychology Today* interview, Dr. Brett Ford, a researcher at the University of Toronto, observed,

> Ironically, it may be helpful to *not* try to control our emotions. If we just accept our emotional experiences and let them run their natural course, they can end more quickly.
>
> This is why emotional acceptance can be a particularly powerful strategy of emotion regulation—it can help you feel better, partly because you don't perpetuate your negative emotions. The goal shouldn't be to get rid of or stifle all emotions. It's to try to have them to the right degree and in the right context and to recover more quickly afterward.[3]

FAITH AND FEELINGS ARE NOT MUTUALLY EXCLUSIVE

I told you earlier about the emotional battles my husband has faced. One of the tactics the Enemy used against him? He turned sad into ashamed.

When Zac faced his initial bout with depression, the first lie he had to fight was wondering which sin he had committed to land him in this place. Certainly, sin can lead you into depression and anxiety and all sorts of negative feelings, but often that's not the case. As he scoured his life, he found no obvious sin, except for overserving and refusing to rest. But how quickly we think that if we are going through difficulty, it must be our fault. And if that is the case, then the feelings that go with the difficult seasons, like sadness or fear or anger, feel more like judgments than gifts.

Zac found a little book, and it sat next to his bed for a year. It was called *Christians Get Depressed Too.*[4] He needed to know that.

Maybe you feel guilty because you feel sad so often. Maybe you feel guilty because you feel happy so often and your friends don't. We are certainly great at feeling one emotion: guilt!

Apparently it's not enough that we are tangled up in our feelings. We have to add another conflict to the mix: the voice of judgment telling us we "shouldn't feel that way."

As I've already noted, for most of my life, control has been my go-to tactic for dealing with uncomfortable emotions, partly because I believed that as a good Christian, I shouldn't be feeling those emotions to begin with. I thought if I believed that God was enough, then I wouldn't be afraid, then I wouldn't be angry, then I wouldn't be worried. Part of that is true. The more we believe God, how good He is, how real He is, how capable and powerful He is, the less we worry and the more we trust Him and the less we spin. But this is not some kind of cruel game where I pay Him with gritted-teeth-non-emotive faith and He reciprocates with peaceful, easy feelings.

You can feel all your feelings and not sin. And you can feel all your feelings and sin. In chapter 12, we will talk about the choices we have for dealing with our emotions and the distinction between our struggles and our sin. But feeling them isn't a sin. And I'm sorry if this book is the first time you're hearing that.

As I've studied the emotional life of God the Father, the Son, and the Holy Spirit, I've become pretty angry that most of my life I've been taught that feeling difficult feelings indicated a lack of faith. Because God feels deeply and often, as we saw in chapter 4. It's worth repeating that God Himself expresses emotions. He gets angry and becomes disappointed and even afraid, as is evident in the anguish of Jesus in the Garden of Gethsemane. And He obviously feels all those things without sin. So why had no one ever taught me how to feel? If God created these feelings and they seemed to be relevant to so much of life and our decisions, why was this news to me?

I'll confess that despite all the work I've done these past three years, sometimes still there's a part of me that feels all the messy things and there's another part of me judging that I feel all these

Grace to Feel: A Personal Story

My mom walked into my room and asked, "How are you doing?"

"Good," I said and then tried to push her out the door. In my mind, emotions are weakness, so I tend to suppress them. She didn't buy it and came in anyway. Slowly, I began to open up about my feelings of loneliness and betrayal.

"Caroline," she said, "you need to learn how to cry and allow yourself grace to feel your emotions." She sat at the end of my bed and put her arms around me. The tears released within me.

Those tears helped me process and grow in the hard.

In that season of my life, my mom became my best friend because she always made me talk. She not only helped me feel safe in expressing my feelings but also helped me know I am not alone in them.

—Caroline, age eighteen

messy things. That part of me that judges is the part of me that's wearing me out. God hasn't put that judgment on me; I put it on myself. And possibly, the Enemy has helped.

That part of us that judges everything we're feeling? We think it's God. But it's shame. And shame is an exhausting companion.

God, by contrast, is the ideal companion, one who wants to replace our shame and exhaustion with His delight and strength. He is looking for a relationship with you and with me. Despite what you may have been taught, our emotions aren't symptoms of sin or a lack of faith. Our emotions are meant to grow our faith, meant to lead us into deeper relationship with the One who made us and created all these emotions.

Untangling our messy mass of feelings will require us to stop seeing them as unhelpful or even sinful, so that we can learn to steward them well. I want us to move from judging what we feel to just feeling it. **We waste so much energy scrutinizing our feelings rather than just feeling what we need to feel.** We can change, I promise, but it will take time and intention.

HOW WE BEGIN TO HEAL

Pause.

Give yourself permission.

Look back.

Persist.

That's how we feel our feelings in an effective and life-giving way. That's how we start to heal the previous versions of ourselves that are ready to finally grow up.

Soon after I started working through this process, I called my counselor and said, "I'm doing the work. I'm feeling the feelings. Really, you'd be very proud. But I'm noticing that the same dumb feelings keep rising to the surface, over and over again. Is there any hope for me?"

Somewhere along the way, I'd picked up the expectation that if I did a good job feeling a certain feeling, then the next feeling that came along would be a more desirable feeling to feel.

You can imagine my disappointment when I realized this wasn't the case.

"Jennie," Dr. C said, in his endlessly empathetic tone, "how long did it take you to get here?" By "here," he meant "this emotional state you're in."

"About forty years," I said, knowing exactly where he was going.

"Yeah," he said. "It's going to take you a minute to get out."

If you find yourself *still* feeling anxious, *still* feeling dejected, *still* feeling melancholy, *still* feeling afraid, remember that progress takes time to run its course. But we'll get there. Eventually, it will feel natural to feel what we feel and boldly move on.

In the meantime, as you see evidence of an earlier version of you showing up, the version who was shut down at age ten, the version who was left out at age twelve, the version who was traumatized at age fifteen, the version who was insecure at age twenty-one, take a lesson from my brilliant sister Katie and simply invite that part of you in.

I see you.

And I want you to know that you're welcome here.

No sudden moves. No rash judgments. Compassion.

11

YOU ARE NOT ALONE IN THIS

NOTICE

NAME

FEEL

SHARE

CHOOSE

When I knew I wanted to write a book on feelings and emotions, I did what I always do whenever I'm about to launch a new project: I gathered some of the smartest people I know into a conference room in Dallas and asked them to weigh in on the subject. Some of the people in the room were from IF:Gathering, people who are part of my everyday life. And some were from outside that ring, people I respect and invite into our circle as often as I can.

One of the individuals who joined us had recently suffered some severe losses in life as a result of sinful personal behavior. She had lost her job, her ministry, her reputation—almost lost her family as well. She was openly repentant, and because for years she has been a trusted friend and fellow creative, I invited her to come.

At the start of the meeting, everyone reintroduced themselves to the rest of the people in the room, and my friend shared what was happening in her life. Then my teammate Chloe looked at her and in front of the entire group said, "Wow, I just want to say that I'm so glad you decided to come."

She went on, but as soon as there was a natural break, I said, "Actually, Chloe, given what we're about to talk about with this new project, would you be willing to say how you *feel* about her being here?"

Chloe teared up.

This person I care deeply for teared up.

Everyone in the room teared up, because all of us suspected that whatever was about to come out of Chloe's mouth represented exactly how we felt.

She then looked directly into this woman's eyes and said, "I feel proud for you that you chose to come, that you chose to share all that with us."

That one line, that one sentiment, altered the tenor of the entire day. In that moment, Chloe's words touched something deep within our friend, which then released her to serve in full.

WHERE TO BEGIN

I was joking with a friend the other day about how over the past few months, it seems like I've been plopped down in a kindergarten class on emotions. On a near daily basis, I'm still saying the wrong thing, leading with thoughts instead of feelings, sticking my foot all the way into my mouth. But I'm messing up *better*. Or at least I know it when I mess up now.

I tell you all this because I want to remind you that there is no shame in beginning something new. Think back to the last time you tried a new sport or started a new hobby or learned to speak a new language. It's *rough* at first, right? Ever visited a country you've never been to before and wondered how you were ever going to figure out the public transportation? It takes a minute, so you give yourself a minute.

Same thing applies here.

When learning to express to another living human being how we're feeling, we're going to trip and fall. We're going to mislabel our feelings from time to time. We're going to step in it once in a while. It's okay. You will get better at this as you go.

First, make sure you are trusting someone safe with your feelings. Maybe mention you are reading this book and that it might be a little awkward as you are learning. My husband laughs because as I've been working on this project, I have been telling him every little feeling I'm feeling, even the stupid ones. He has had to withhold judgment, knowing I am hyperfocusing on a healthier practice of sharing them.

He told me today, "I have had to not react to it all and listen and comfort without freaking out that you are feeling all these feelings!"

It's a good idea to view this as a season of building a healthier relationship with your emotions and not as a landing spot where you will forever name every insignificant mood or feeling flying through your head.

For now, here's what I want you to do: After you go through the paces of noticing, naming, and feeling a feeling regarding a situation you're facing, open your mouth in the presence of someone you know and preferably like and practice saying a few simple words, "I feel _____," and insert an emotion there.

That's it.

"I feel . . . *happy.*"

"I feel . . . *overwhelmed.*"

"I feel . . . *grateful.*"

"I feel . . . *concerned.*"

"I feel . . . *confused.*"

"I feel . . . *disillusioned.*"

"I feel . . . *let down.*"

I know this is going to be uncomfortable, but science is clear. When we allow ourselves the space to feel versus think our problems, the right side of our brain lights up. Science shows that when people were "asked to focus on *what* was said—semantics—blood flow velocity went up significantly on the left side of the brain. When participants shifted attention to how it was said—tone of voice, whether happy, sad, anxious, angry or neutral—velocity also went up markedly on the right side of the brain." When you say "I feel _____" you move from the left side of your brain to the right side of your brain. The right part of our brain is the place of connection, empathy, healing, and connection with God and other people.[1]

You've been practicing this concept covertly; now just open your mouth. You won't get it right every time, especially at first, but getting it right isn't even the point. For now, it's enough to get used to hearing yourself say, "I feel . . ."

I know what you're thinking, *How is this helpful? It doesn't change anything. My problems are still my problems, and I have to deal with them regardless of how I or anyone else feels about them.*

It's one thing to have to feel all your feelings, and it's a whole other thing to have to share them with people. I get it. It sucks. I feel that way every time I'm about to do it. But I never feel that way after I do it. I am always grateful I shared.

To be truly seen, soothed, safe, and not alone in the pain heals you in ways you can't believe unless you have felt it.

For those of us who were taught we shouldn't burden other people with our problems, it may help to remember that God does more than encourage us to share our difficulties with one another; He commands us: "Bear one another's burdens, and so fulfill the law of Christ."[2] Fulfill the law of Christ? That sounds intense. It sounds important. It sounds necessary. But we can't bear what others don't share, and the reverse is also true.

Have you ever been sitting across from someone who tears up and nods as you share about the difficult things in your life? Their response makes you cry and frees you to release burdens you didn't even know you were carrying.

THE COMFORT OF A BURDEN SHARED

When Jesus says, "My yoke is easy, and my burden is light,"[3] He's not saying life is going to be easy. In other passages, He says there is trouble in this world and He calls us to pick up our crosses.[4] The burden is light because He is with us, and His presence and comfort and friendship make life easier and sweeter. He makes suffering easier because He never leaves us and will carry it along with us.

One of the most emotional moments in Jesus's life was after the death of His good friend Lazarus. Days after His friend has passed, Jesus arrives at the home Lazarus shared with his two sisters, also good friends of Jesus. Martha is angry, and she lets Him know it: "If you had been here, my brother would not have died."[5]

How many times have we been angry at God but scared to say so? Jesus did not shame Martha. He comforted her and issued a greater hope than an earthly healing: "I am the resurrection and the life. Whoever believes in me, though he die, yet shall he live, and everyone who lives and believes in me shall never die."[6]

He comforts Martha with the hope that only He can give. Then He comes to Mary, the other sister of Lazarus, and she falls at His feet, weeping. Scripture says Jesus named that He was deeply troubled and moved by the weeping of Mary, and He wept with her.[7] This is the only human who has ever walked the face of the earth who actually had the power to solve the problem of death, both in the moment and for eternity. And yet Fix-It Jesus does not show up here. Feel-It Jesus shows up and weeps with His friend who is weeping.

Why?

He knew He would raise Lazarus from the dead. He knew He would fix the problem both temporarily and eternally for all of them. Yet, in Martha's anger and Mary's grief, Jesus does not correct them; He comforts them.

In this scene, He models for us what it means to live out Paul's instruction in Romans to "rejoice with those who rejoice; mourn with those who mourn."[8]

I don't know if you've ever felt grief like Mary's. If you have, you know.

There's nothing to say.

There's nothing to do.

You only want people around you feeling the pain with you. Something about mourning with those who mourn helps when nothing else can and nothing else will. And Jesus knew that.

SHARING ACTUALLY HEALS US

If I hadn't done the scientific research on this, I wouldn't believe that mourning with those who mourn actually helps and heals us. But the more we learn about how the brain changes in response to traumatic events, the more we see how the opposite is also true: Sharing our story in safe, connected relationships can heal the brain.

Just today, someone sent me a video of what I've read about a hundred times in the research: neural pathways reconnecting after being broken. It's a real thing. You can google it and see for yourself. A brain making new connections where trauma has severed and damaged certain parts. It looks like little strings working really hard to find their way back to each other. As you watch it, you think they're never going to make it. They're never going to reconnect. They're never going to heal.

But our little neuron buddies—they fight toward each other and they find each other. I cried when I saw it, because it's why I'm writing this book. What good are a million feelings if they don't bring healing and wholeness? The way they bring healing and wholeness is connection with each other. And with God. As we share our sadness, our fear, our worry with people who are safe, who see us, and who comfort us, we heal. Again, the science has told me this a hundred times, but it's hard to believe it can really change things. But it does.

Yesterday I sat with a group of dear friends as one of them cried and listed off a series of angst-ridden circumstances that she can't escape. I've watched this friend carrying these things for several weeks and known her heart might burst, but we just hadn't had time to air it all out. She finally unloaded with all of us listening patiently and quietly, without interrupting.

Now, mind you, I wanted to interrupt her. Words kept coming up in my throat as she spoke, wanting to redirect all the hard into something hopeful. But I've learned better. We sat in the hard with her, and no one fixed anything.

Sure, there is a time and place for follow-up questions, suggested solutions, and actions you or the other person might take. But generally that isn't actually what people need. Most people know the right answers. We don't have a knowledge problem. **The problem is that we feel unsafe and unloved and unseen. We won't move toward healing until those wounds are addressed.**

When I saw that friend again later that day, I asked a simple question: "Do you feel better?" She giggled for the first time in weeks, heaved a sigh, and said, "Yeah, I do."

Her relaxed posture and laughter confirmed once more what both the Bible and a bazillion scientists have told us: Sharing puts us on a path toward healing.

FEELING OUT LOUD

With all this in mind, I have a challenge for you: The next time you're in a conversation with someone, instead of responding to a story or update with some sort of enthusiastic declaration like, "That's great!" or, worse still, with any statement that begins with the phrase *"I think . . . ,"* force your lips to form the words *"I feel."*

Then tell the person how you feel. That's it! Nothing more.

A few examples:

A friend rushes into the coffee shop fifteen minutes late, gives you a quick squeeze hello, and then blows through a whole explanation about how the babysitter didn't show and the neighbor was unavailable and she almost ran out of gas and blah, blah, blah.

What do you say? "I feel compassionate that it was such a wild start to your day and happy you are here now!"

Your teenage son opens up to you about a fight with a friend. Instead of asking what he did wrong, lead with, "I feel grateful you feel safe to tell me this and sad that this was so hurtful."

The stylist who cuts your hair confides that she recently caught her partner in an affair. What do you say? "I feel so sad with you that you're having to walk through this."

Your date or boyfriend sincerely compliments you in front of a whole table of dinner guests. Later, when it's just the two of you, what do you say? "I feel overwhelmed and loved by your words tonight. Thank you."

Let me say again that in asking you to practice sharing your feelings with people, I'm not suggesting that it is never appropriate to share solutions. Ideas. Explanations. Thoughts. What I'm saying is that *we don't need practice sharing those things*. **We are already experts in sharing our thoughts! What do we need practice with? Leading with emotion.**

So, all of that is step one: Start with "I feel . . ."

Step two: Ask for an "I feel . . ." statement in response.

You read me right. In addition to responding to people with "I feel" statements, try *soliciting* them once in a while. The next time you face a quandary of some sort—some situation is bugging you, some conversation has left you feeling frustrated or weak, some burden is breaking your back—approach someone you trust, whether that person is a family member, a friend, or a beloved server at your favorite café, and say, "Hey, can I tell you something and you tell me how it makes you feel?"

Admittedly, that construction is a little contrived and clunky, but so far it's the best I've been able to do. And the point of the whole thing is preserved, which is to invite someone you know and like to express how something you've said makes them feel.

Candid Conversations: A Personal Story

Growing up in the home of an addict, I experienced daily emotional volatility. My mom, sister, and I were all trying to make sense of the dysfunction in our own way. My way of coping? Absorbing whatever emotion was floating around me. Maybe by absorbing it, I could understand it, perhaps protect myself from it, or—best case—control it!

I became a professional at conforming to the emotional state of people around me until my body physically couldn't take it. I started counseling at a young age and continued off and on for decades. But every few years, my physical body would collapse beneath me, often in the form of debilitating anxiety.

Finally, in my early thirties, I pressed deeper than I ever had before to let God uncover why part of me wanted to curl up on the floor of my closet and stay there forever. Through intensive counseling, medication, and incredibly candid conversations with the people I loved, I started to really live again. It's like life is in full color now!

Now, I know you think what you've just done—the solicitation—is the hard part, but it isn't. The hard part comes now, when you have to keep them on the feelings train and not let them jump to the thinking track.

Case in point: Several weeks ago I showed up at one of my small groups for our weekly meeting. I hurriedly hugged a few necks and then beelined it for my seat.

As I've mentioned already, Zac's business, one he'd worked pas-

Many days I think, *Can all this digging deep be over now?* It's exhausting work to tell God, yourself, and others the truth and then wait in that momentary pause to know if you're safe and how the person across from you will respond. But in the presence of safe relationships, that's where real healing began for me. Unlearning the pattern of absorbing emotions that are not mine, discerning what I really feel, and allowing myself to feel my own feelings is a daily fight. But now that I know what it's like, I never want to go back.

I am believing and praying that this book could be a new beginning for you too. You were made distinct from other people, loved by God, and given your own set of experiences and emotions. Press in and feel them. Then may God give us both the strength to feel fully, express our emotions with courage, and continue through to the other side and learn what God wants us to experience.

—Chloe, age thirty-two

sionately and for so long to build, was crumbling before our eyes, I was dealing with my own pressure-cooker-like experience at work, one of our kids was veering way off the rails and seemed destined for a crash—you get the idea. I had feelings to *share*.

Now, I love the people in my small group. They are full of wisdom while still being humble to their core. We say the truth together and hold each other accountable and pray. But for all the benefits they bring to my life, I wouldn't call them the most emotionally expressive friends I've ever had. (They are laughing as they read this because they know it is true.) In fact, our husbands, who meet together weekly and text daily, are much more emotional than the female side of this group.

We just don't make a habit of talking about mushy things like emotions. But I had plans for their lives on this day, plans involving feeling all the feelings.

We exchanged pleasantries for a while, and then I asked if I could give an update on what was going on in the Allen household and see what feelings were elicited in the group. Over the years, I've learned that sometimes you have to ask explicitly for what you need. So before I gave my little spiel, I said, "Listen, I know you guys are super-smart with hundreds of years of lived experience among you. You've seen it all and done it all, but I'm not wanting to know what you think about what I'm about to tell you. I want to know how you *feel*."

They nodded indulgently. I unloaded to them about every last one of the various situations I'd been hauling around in my soul's overstuffed backpack, then exhaled the breath I'd been holding the entire time and looked around the room. Nobody had fled in terror—a good sign. But also true: Nobody was saying a word.

"Well," I said, "what do you think?"

One woman started to respond, "Well, I think—"

"Wait, wait," I said. "I didn't mean that. I meant, what do you *feel*?"

She took another run at it. "Okay, well, let's see. I . . . *feel* . . . proud of you."

Reflexively, I smiled.

"I feel proud of you for telling us," she said. "And for walking through such a difficult season with Zac with grace."

Another spoke up. "I feel sad it is so hard for you two right now."

Another, "Yes. I agree. And I would add that I feel compassion for your situation. None of those circumstances are easy to face, but you two are facing them."

Tears sprang to my eyes. The usual quick advice turned to empathy, and my soul felt understood and comforted. Seen. Soothed. Safe.

It was just like I'd experienced with Dr. C during that one-on-one counseling session, but, *of course,* Dr. C will say the right thing. What I hadn't been sure of was whether real people, normal people, people out here in the wild, could or would say the right thing too—not the fix-it thing but the feel-it thing. What I'd wanted to know was whether this stuff worked without the presence of paid professionals.

It does.

REMEMBER THE GOAL: TO *CONNECT*

A few months ago, my son Cooper was having a rough day. I heard him breaking down in the bathroom, and when I poked my head around the door and asked, "What's up, buddy?" he explained through sobs that he'd been left out of a get-together with his friends.

It was clear to me how he was feeling, but I have to tell you, I was so stoked when he looked at me and said, "Mom, I feel sad."

"Of course you are. That hurts. I feel so sad with you."

And I did.

Of course I did.

And on some occasions, it would have been right to just let us both sit in the sad. But here's the thing: Resilience grows as we notice, name, feel, and share our feelings and in doing so learn that we are seen, soothed, and safe.

Cooper is right in the middle of his teenage years, and there's drama behind every bush. The fact was, he'd been left out before. We've cried these same tears before.

I hugged my kid and then pulled back and said, "Hey, buddy, how has it turned out in the past when you have been left out?"

His eyes darted back and forth and then brightened. "I *have* been left out before. It was okay. I was okay." And then he looked at me and said, "Plus, I always have y'all."

Yes, buddy, you always have us. I want my son to feel safe to be sad and safe to be left out. The more he experiences that safety and us and Jesus in it all with him, the more his soul will heal.

The hard stuff actually is building us into who we are, as the apostle Paul knew so well:

We also glory in tribulations, knowing that tribulation produces perseverance; and perseverance, character; and character, hope. Now hope does not disappoint, because the love of God has been poured out in our hearts by the Holy Spirit who was given to us.[9]

Hope doesn't disappoint us, because we have that rope of emotions connecting us, pulling us into each other and into God. The gift of feeling and moving through the dadgum middle of it— together. It is agonizing beauty. **Feelings don't heal when we ignore them; they heal when we are wrapped up by the people we love in the middle of them.**

Resilience, maturity, connection, character, and hope growing right before my eyes as we sat on a bathroom floor being sad . . . together.

12

WHAT TO DO WITH
WHAT YOU FEEL

NOTICE

NAME

FEEL

SHARE

CHOOSE

In high school, I dated a golfer, so I used to watch a lot of golf. And my favorite golfer to watch was Tiger Woods. I often thought how glad I was not to be a golfer on the PGA tour in the years Tiger was in his heyday. How miserable to be an excellent golfer but happen to be alive and golfing when he was on the scene. Nobody cared how good the second-best player was, or even who it was, as it was all about Tiger. He creamed the whole field for a moment in time. We all believed that as long as he lived and played, he would be the best. With all that talent, how could he not?

But Tiger was complicated, like all humans. He had a dark side, and it was twisting him in knots on the inside. He kept it hidden, until he couldn't. How does the personal life of a golfer seep so deeply into his game? Because despite our best efforts to keep them in a box on the shelf, our emotions inevitably affect the rest of our life. Tiger's golf game fell apart because of his tangled-up personal and emotional life.

We all want to believe we can compartmentalize things to avoid dealing with the messy stuff. We convince ourselves that . . .

We can be a great worker.

We can be a great parent.

We can be a great spouse.

We can be a great college student.

We can be a great Christian.

And yet still be a disaster emotionally.

Nope. Emotions affect everything.

We all want to be emotionally healthy, so now what?

We notice it and name it and feel it and share it, and then what?

What if it still feels like it may take us under?

We've come to the point in this process—and we'll come to it probably dozens of times every day—where, once we notice what we feel, name what we feel, actually feel it and share it, we have to decide what to do with it.

Even if you think you aren't doing anything with your feelings, you are.

Maybe up to this point you've stuffed them, ignored them, put the tangled-up mess of them in a box on the shelf of your heart. But they're still there.

Or maybe you've let your emotions run wild and allowed them to control your day, your year, your life.

Either way, you've made a decision, whether intentionally or not. But you have another option: You can feel the emotions, share them with the people you love, and let them draw you closer to the God who wants to carry your burdens. As the Bible tells us, "Cast all your anxiety on him because he cares for you."[1]

Choosing to engage this process leads to wholeheartedness. It leads to connection. It leads to the kind of life God built for us and wants for us.

FIRST, WE CHOOSE TO DO THIS WITH GOD

But let's talk about what doing this with God actually looks like. Because there's nothing worse than when someone tosses out a Bible verse like it's a lifeline and you can't quite figure out why it's not working for you. As if everyone else only needs a Bible verse and their crazy heart calms down and they're not afraid anymore.

Let's look at a moment where engaging the process actually happened with Jesus and His people.

In Matthew 8, the disciples and Jesus are on a boat and a wild storm comes up and scares the disciples to death. Jesus, however, is asleep in the bottom of the boat. Now, obviously, these disciples have some anxiety in this instant and probably can't believe that their rabbi is sound asleep in the middle of this storm. So they go and wake Him and say, "Lord, save us! We're going to drown!"

In this moment, Jesus says, "Hey, I have this." He takes care of the problem.

But in the future, the disciples will face many problems that He does not resolve so neatly. They'll be imprisoned. They will be beaten and rejected. Peter will be crucified. John will be exiled to an island. The storms will come with even more intensity than they did on that day at sea.

But . . .

Something was totally, utterly different in how they handled those storms. The disciples went from being people pleasers, competing for honor, doubting themselves and God, afraid of a little storm . . . to people who would give their lives for this God.

What changed?

How can the emotional state of these men be so completely different a few years later?

Because they walked with Him.

They talked with Him.

They served with Him.

They learned from Him.

They became like Him.

They were filled by Him.

And as that happened, day in and day out, over years, they trusted Him. And they went from people afraid to die in a boat with Him to people willing to lay down their lives because of Him. Because He cared for them. Just as He cares for you.

Faith isn't summoned; it grows. It grows because of a relationship, not your willpower.

It grows because of the desperate nights when you can't quit crying and you think nobody sees you, but He is with you and you feel it and you know it.

Because of the waiting rooms, where it seems like hours before the doctor comes out to tell you if your loved one is okay or not, but He is with you. He cares for you.

Because of the injustice at work, where you are misunderstood and you did nothing wrong, yet He knows and He is with you. He cares for you.

Because of the bliss you feel on a day when the sun is shining and the playlist is right and you are walking and talking with Him and He's there.

Because . . . He is there.

With you.

There.

A relationship with God—it changes everything. He untangles the chaotic knots in our souls—but probably not in the way that we expected and maybe not in the way we learned, which was to pretend that they aren't there and tell ourselves that everything's okay and chastise ourselves because if we just believed God enough, we wouldn't be so sad or worried.

He untangles the knots through seasons of tears and raw honesty and running again and again back to Him . . . because He cares for us. He wants all of us. He wants to know it all.

So we choose to notice and name and feel and share—and in every step along that path, we invite Jesus into it. We tell Him all of it.

My prayer life is largely a lot of feelings I am running to Him with. I run to Him and tell Him when I can't because of a kid who is anxious, when I am so mad at Zac I want to punch him, when I am sad I am left out of a gathering of friends, when I am giddy from watching Him change someone's life.

Joy connects us to God, giver of all the good stuff.

Fear connects us to God, our safe place.

Anger connects us to God, our avenger.

Sadness connects us to God, our God who understands rejection. Even feelings like guilt connect us to God, the One who died for our guilt and shame and sin.

I wish this weren't the way. I wish my relationship with God was not built through tears and raw emotion. But then again, I wouldn't trade it. Because I don't see another way. These feelings that all my life I've been afraid to feel are the tether God's got wrapped around my waist, pulling me in closer and closer and closer to Him. If I let Him and don't fight it by controlling, coping, or concealing, it's scary, but I find my home and comfort in Him.

And you can too.

NEXT, WE CHOOSE THE RAW UNVARNISHED TRUTH

You know who is good at this? Gen Z. (If you're one of my Gen Z friends, I'm going to talk about you for a minute here.)

I've seen God's healing power at work in the lives of other people who choose to let their emotions draw them close to Him, and I'm convinced that doing so—getting real and authentic and raw with God about both our struggles and our sin—is exactly what will help this next generation, and all of us really, untangle the twisted mess inside.

Several years ago, before I knew Gen Z was called Gen Z, I saw a shift in the rooms where I was speaking. The first time it happened, I was at Breakaway (an on-campus Bible study) at Texas A&M University in 2018. I've written about this event before, so I won't go into the details here, but to sum up what happened that night, I'd say that a collective confession unfolded, right before my eyes. At the end of my talk, I asked everyone in attendance to set down the burden they'd been carrying, the weighty sin that they were hiding, the thing that nobody in their life—their roommates, their family members, their friends—knew about.

We don't keep secrets; secrets keep us. And I knew that until those students admitted what they were keeping secret, they would be stunted in their spiritual growth.

So I asked, "What secret are you keeping? What sin do you need to confess?"

And before I fully understood what was happening, kids were standing up from their seats one at a time and then six or ten or twenty at a time, literally yelling out their sin. In front of the people they liked and loved and wanted to be liked and loved by, they were shouting, "Pornography!" "Sex!" "Binge drinking!" "Suicidal thoughts!" "Eating disorder!" "Cutting!"

It wouldn't stop. Once one person was honest, everyone felt permission to be honest, and as I stood there, mic in hand, tears streaming down my face, I shook my head in awe.

Every time I raised the mic to my lips to close the time of confession, another ten kids would shout out their sin or struggle. As if they didn't want to miss the chance to say it out loud. To be free of it.

Months later, I spoke at Baylor University and the same thing happened. I spoke at the Passion conference in Atlanta to sixty-five thousand students. Same thing. An entire generation was telling me, telling each other, telling God that they were sick of being in bondage.

They were ready to live free.

Are you?

Freedom always costs us something. It costs us appearances,

possibly our reputation. It costs us our control because as we turn everything over to God, we learn that He says how it all goes. It costs us our unhealthy addictions that we think are sources of comfort but actually are binding us and blinding us.

Last week, while I was working on this part of the book, I received a news alert on my phone with this title: "Teen girls are experiencing record-high levels of sadness and violence: CDC." I clicked on the link and saw this lead-in: "According to new CDC data released today, nearly 3 in 5 (57%) U.S. teen girls felt persistently sad or hopeless in 2021—double that of boys, representing a nearly 60% increase and the highest level reported over the past decade."[2]

Three in five. That's nearly 60 percent of all teenage girls, a number that's just way too high. We can look at a stat like that and say that we've got a mental-health crisis on our hands. And we have said that. Because we do.

But here's what a figure like that says to me: If there is a crisis to be found here, it's a crisis of *connection* at its core. In that same CDC article, the finger was pointing at social media. And at the devastating effects that the Covid-19 pandemic had on us all. And at the trend line these past few years toward less in-person contact and more virtual reality in our lives.

It's so broken. We all know it. And to some extent, we know why.

If we're spending more time each day all alone, staring at a screen, absorbing everyone else's curated perfection, of course we're going to feel persistently sad and hopeless—not just teenage girls, but all of us. Negativity and disaster are everywhere we look. Of course we're going to look to food or alcohol or anything to help us. We'll try *anything* that promises relief.

But something is happening with this generation that is radical and that no one saw coming: The ones who love Jesus are *zealots*. The ones who love Jesus *really* love Jesus. They throw off their sin and struggles faster than anyone I have seen so they can follow Jesus with reckless abandon. They want God. And it isn't even complicated for them. They just want more of Him.

When Christians were going to church just because they were supposed to, ambivalence grew. But this generation is saying, "You know what? No one is pressuring me to do this, but I'm going to follow Jesus, and I don't care what it costs." And God is moving. We need to be looking at them, and we need to be learning from them, and we also need to be giving them the things they need to succeed. We need to disciple them.

As I was working on this book, I saw on Instagram that a revival had broken out at a chapel service at Asbury University. Students were lingering there to be with God, day after day. One of my Gen Z buddies reached out and said, "Let's go, Jennie. Let's go see it." We left for Asbury that day, and it was everything you think and more.

Simple.

No plan.

Prayer, worship, and confession.

Just students bringing their pillows and sleeping bags to stay in the presence of God through the night. They didn't want to leave. And so they didn't. They just stayed.

This younger generation wants God. And they are in a full-on mental-health crisis. Both are true. And I believe that both are connected.

Often, we want God only when we are desperate. Are you reading these words feeling desperate? Being desperate is not only a problem; it is also an opportunity. Desperate people knock on doors they wouldn't otherwise knock on, to get help they wouldn't otherwise need. And we have a God who answers: "Ask, and it will be given to you; seek, and you will find; knock, and it will be opened to you."[3]

Jesus is talking about the hope of Himself—salvation, forgiveness. Knock and it is yours. And then we work out the rest with fear and trembling as we make our way eternally home.

Jesus is their hope.

Jesus is our hope.

But we must be honest about where we are and our desperate need for God.

WE ALL GET tangled up, wound up, and worked up from time to time. There is grace for that. I want you to imagine we're sitting across the table from each other and you're telling me just how worked up you are and how flooded with fear or anger or sadness you are. I want you to see my face. I'm not judging you. I'm not looking down on you. My face is compassionate and empathetic, and I'm not leaving the room.

Sometimes the "truth [that] will set you free"[4] is saying to God and others what is true about the state of your heart. God's word sets free the parts of us that need it, and we have to be truthful about where we are struggling. Even if it feels impossible to say out loud . . .

Confessing suicidal ideation.

Confessing bitterness from an unwanted divorce.

Confessing gripping fear that you won't ever get married.

Confessing grief that you still have from losing a parent.

Confession is to speak what is true. Sometimes what is true is that life is difficult because you are choosing sin. You're sleeping with a boyfriend, abusing alcohol, sucked into porn. You are choosing something more than God, and it's made you emotionally sick.

But sometimes the truth about what we are struggling with is not sin. Many times, we emotionally hit a wall because life just sucks and our bodies are broken and they just don't function how we wish they could.

Because it is all so broken. But the Bible issues hope for the brokenness.

"Those who sow in tears shall reap with shouts of joy!"[5]

"Blessed are those who mourn, for they shall be comforted."[6]

"I have told you these things," Jesus said, "so that in me you may have peace. In this world you will have trouble. But take heart! I have overcome the world."[7]

God isn't afraid of the brokenness, and we shouldn't be either. He has a plan to set us free—in those college kids' lives, in Zac's life, in my life, and in yours too.

BUT WHAT IF WE ARE STILL DROWNING?

We run to God, and we run to our people. And we take all the information, and we decide what we need. We assess whether our response to our feelings is healthy and reasonable in a given situation, such as having heartache over a broken relationship, or whether we've become tangled up in unhealthy or even sinful behaviors, such as isolating ourselves in hopes of protection from future pain or trying to bind up our fractured heart by sleeping around.

There's not a right way to feel sad; you just feel sad. However, what you choose to do with sadness sure can screw up your life. You can try to drink yourself back to happiness, or you can connect with others and God.

Remember the train image from chapter 4? This is where our wills must decide what to do with our feelings. What will our feelings lead us toward in life? Are we going to seek help from

Trusting Our Emotions to God: A Personal Story

I can still hear the line "Emotions are excuses" being yelled at me by my dad, who knew no other way to parent. The generations who came before us didn't know any other way than to stuff, numb, and bypass one's fragile emotions.

I carried that line with me when I lost my virginity to a sexually manipulative guy at age thirteen. I carried that line with me when I numbed the pain with alcohol and drugs at sixteen and eighteen. I carried that line as I stayed in an abusive marriage for far too long. "Emotions are excuses," I reminded myself. "Just be strong. Stick it out."

Then I fell in love with the God who created me and my emotions. And now I know the truth: He is close to the brokenhearted. Not only that, but He revives His sons and daughters who feel completely crushed.[8]

Your emotions and mine aren't afterthoughts to God; they're priorities, and I believe He does His best work when we surrender them to Him. What a really good heavenly Father we have.

—Toni, age thirty-two

God and others regularly? Are we going to be consumed by our rage or despair? Or are we going to choose to face all of it and let our emotions lead us to greater places of empathy and connection?

Much of the time, we just need to go through the first four phases—noticing, naming, feeling, and sharing—without judgment and allow our feelings to connect us to God and to people. It's okay to lean into those feelings for the moment and let them do the work they were meant for. They're true and real, and it's actually healthy for you to feel them.

But sometimes a feeling that should last for maybe a few days turns into a feeling that lasts a few years, or we find that a certain feeling repeatedly propels us toward unhealthy behavior. And while confession moves us toward healing, there are other decisions that need to be made.

Do we need counseling?

Do we need to get out of sinful ruts?

Do we need to address hurts haunting us from childhood?

Do we need to heal from circumstances beyond our control?

Do we need to learn new healthy patterns for dealing with our emotional outbursts?

Do we need marriage counseling?

Do we need a new way to do life in a healthier way?

Is it a mood that will pass in a day or two? Or is it a season that will last weeks or months?

Or have our emotions turned into strongholds that are controlling us and we're no longer in control?

Imagine all your various emotions are the ocean and you're standing on the shore. Sometimes the waves are hitting your ankles or maybe even your knees. You're just observing and experiencing the emotions.

But other times, those emotions sweep you out into the deep. Maybe for a swim, and it's a lovely day.

Or maybe it's a riptide, and it's taking you under and out so far that you really need help.

This part of the process is not black-and-white; it's a journey of discovering what you are feeling and what you and your community think you need. If noticing, naming, feeling, and sharing have led you and your people to conclude that your emotions are telling you it's time to make a change, in the next chapter, you'll find a number of ideas for how to make that choice.

PASTORING OUR SOULS

Over the past few years, I've started seeing myself as the pastor of my own soul. For so long, I was waiting for someone out there to come and fix me, someone out there to come and heal me, and someone out there to make things right.

As a follower of Jesus, I'm well aware that in terms of eternal redemption, I have no power apart from Christ. I'm also aware that every last one of the calls in Scripture was given with the assumption that I would carry them out in the context of communal life.

But here's what I didn't realize: In light of those two truths, God laid out both a plan and the means. We have hope and healing because of Jesus and all He did, *and* we have the power to change and love and engage and make new decisions because of the Holy Spirit. It's all possible because of His strength in us.

I've learned that nothing is better at helping me make sense of the knots in my soul than asking these two questions, inviting Him in, sometimes hour by hour:

.   .   .

God, what do You want me to know?
God, what do You want me to do?

We will never know the answers to these questions if we don't ask. He is waiting to lead you beside still waters, to shepherd your soul! He's waiting for you to decide you want to be healed.

feeling our way forward

13

DEALING WITH
STUBBORN KNOTS

So often the reason we fall into the emotional traps of controlling our feelings, coping instead of acknowledging our feelings at all, and concealing our feelings is that the memories behind those feelings are so terribly triggering that we're momentarily paralyzed, unsure what to do.

I was talking with a friend about how hard it is to feel hard feelings, and she said, "I have feelings that I'll never be able to fully feel. They're like the thread hanging off my sweater, and if I pull that one thread, the whole sweater will come undone."

It's so true, isn't it? Sometimes it feels like that.

But here's the truth: That sweater needs to come unraveled, because it's keeping exactly *nobody* warm. I told my friend as much. "I hear you, but instead of thinking of those unfelt feelings as a nice, comfy sweater, better to think of them as a knotted rope that's hanging around your neck. Only good will come from untangling it."

Sometimes our heavy feelings are justified—maybe we've experienced a hard diagnosis or broken marriage or the abandonment of a parent or financial devastation—and sometimes they aren't even necessarily rooted in reality. But either way, your feelings are real and there are some tangible steps you can take to navigate them in a healthy way.

Whether the thing you don't want to deal with is feeling like you've let someone down, or feeling like you're not measuring up, or feeling like you'll never be able to change, or feeling like your life is destined to be disappointing, or feeling like you'll always be misunderstood, or feeling like you'll never find a friend group that will stay loyal to you, or feeling like you'll never be worthy of love, or feeling any of a million different doom-forecasting feelings or things that are even more concrete and inescapable . . .

What I want to say to you as someone who has been emotionally stuck in life more times than I care to count—as someone who *still today* occasionally gets twisted up in her emotions, as if she's tangled in the leash of an especially rambunctious dog—**there are times when simple awareness can help us straighten things out and extricate ourselves. And there are times when more help is needed.**

Sometimes even when we have felt the pain and let it lead us to Jesus and others, it just still feels like we'll never get free.

You are not crazy.

We all have been there.

But even as we give ourselves permission to feel the truth of all that, and even as we recognize there are no magic solutions, there are tangible things we can do to help loosen those knots.

BEGIN WITH THE BODY

As I have shared, we have been on a mental-health journey not only in our own family but with more than a handful of close friends. And over and over, we've discovered that the feelings we are struggling with are frequently exacerbated by how we're treating—or, more often, mistreating and ignoring—our bodies.

Whenever people reach out, after some initial back-and-forth, Zac and I always suggest they begin the same way: "Go to your doctor," we tell them. "Get a full physical, head to toe."

The fact is that as adults, we are horrible about keeping up with our own physical care. We may be completely obsessive about ensuring that our kids get yearly checkups and that they have access to all the necessary resources to help them grow up healthy and strong. But ask around in your own friendship circle and you'll hear the same stuff I hear in mine:

"A physical? I haven't had one of those in . . . *years*."

"Doctor? My kids have a pediatrician, but I don't go."

"Yeah, we don't have great health insurance. We don't ever go."

I'm not trying to be bossy here, but I'm going to be bossy here. Even if these and every other possible excuse are true for you, table them and go get checked out. Here's why: We change.

Also true: Even if you have no obvious symptoms of disease, dysfunction, or distress, you cannot assume that all is well beneath your skin, my friend. Things are fine until they are not. Am I right?

You would be shocked by what I hear from my friends and family members who finally do as they're told. They come back to me and say the darndest things:

"Jennie, it was my thyroid! My thyroid was all but *shut down*."

"Jennie, I'm in total adrenal failure. That's why I can't get out of bed!"

"Jennie, my blood work was all over the place. Who knew I needed vitamins to live?"

"Jennie, my blood pressure was through the freaking *roof*. No wonder I feel anxious most days."

"Jennie, my hormone panel was completely off. I had no idea."

And many of these were said by young people, in their twenties. We all need to follow this advice.

And to that last point, did you know that the body's endocrine system—our hormonal system—is directly linked to the part of our brain that processes feelings?[1] If you are a woman or man struggling emotionally and have not run a hormone panel in more than twelve months, get yourself to a professional now. If you do not have health insurance, look for a free clinic. In Dallas, our church offers free medical care through several facilities for anyone who doesn't have insurance.

Even if there's nothing measurably wrong in your body, there are so many ways most of us could choose to take better care of ourselves. Sometimes we need medicine for depression and anxiety, and praise God that it exists. But before my primary-care doctor, who is a believer, will prescribe such medications, she has a list of questions about the things we should try first. Here are a few, along with brief notes from me about why each of these questions about our physical and spiritual lives is relevant to our emotional well-being:

- Are you moving your body every day? (Produces serotonin)

- Are you sharing what is difficult with friends and family? (Heals neural pathways)

- How much alcohol are you drinking? (Depletes dopamine)

- Are you eating a balanced diet? (Affects every bodily function we have and therefore our emotional life)

- Are you spending time with Jesus? (Yes, she asks that of patients who are people of faith, because she knows that a connection with Jesus is healing in ways nothing else can be.)

If most of those things are already in order and a patient needs medicine, perhaps to address a chemical issue, she will absolutely prescribe it. Otherwise, she asks patients to try some lifestyle adjustments that are proven to affect our emotional well-being.

So, what follows is a list of things that really do help. It's far from exhaustive, but if you've been wrestling for some time to stay in touch with yourself and effectively feel what you feel or if you're stuck in emotional unhealth, choosing to make these adjustments can be helpful, sometimes life changing. I know this because I've been where you are.

TAKE A BREAK FROM SCREENS

Our emotions are strongest the first time we encounter something. The first time we saw the ocean or the mountains, the first time we saw a baby born—those feelings overwhelm us. But the twelfth time we've seen the ocean, it doesn't have quite the same impact. It's just the way we were built.

So, the first time you heard your parents fight, perhaps you were six years old and crying in your bedroom. But years later, if your parents were fighters and you'd witnessed dozens of fights, you didn't cry anymore. You knew they would make it. Or you would hope so, anyway.

Novelty causes the most extreme emotional reaction.

It's why video-game simulation is one of the ways people train for combat. You think I'm kidding, but this is actually how they train. Because part of our brain can't differentiate between something virtual and something real. So, if you have seen it happen virtually, it's as if it's happened to you. A part of our brain knows the difference. But that training wouldn't work unless part of our brain *didn't* know the difference. As the novelty of watching death and war diminishes, our emotional responses diminish.

Are you tracking with me? This means that in a digital age where we have been exposed to death, sex, tragedies on a daily basis, our emotional reactions are stunted and confused. Novelty has nothing on this generation. We've seen it all thousands of times over, confusing our emotional lives and traumatizing them as well. So, whether you wonder why you can't feel enough when needed or why you feel so anxious when your circumstances aren't so bad or why your child can't seem to get through a day at school, envision how that part of your brain or your child's brain has actually been through all the traumas you've ever seen on a screen.

When I was growing up—before computers, the internet, and iPhones—the only whiff of suffering I got outside immediate friends and family was a vague mention of children starving in China because I didn't eat all my food on my plate.

In just the past three weeks, as I'm writing this, we have seen the faces and learned the names of three nine-year-old children shot in an elementary school. We've seen images of destruction from a tornado that devastated the middle of our country. And if you're a parent, probably one of your children has killed a few people on *Mortal Kombat* or, depending on their age, *LEGO Star Wars: The Video Game.*

With all our screen time, we are numbing ourselves to pain and therefore numbing ourselves to life. We are losing how to feel sad and angry and how to feel wonder and joy. We have seen it all and felt it all and find ourselves just looking for the next hit of adrenaline instead of deep connection in our pain and joy.

So, let's limit it all. News feeds, Twitter and Threads feeds, Tik-Tok feeds. Binge watching on Netflix and YouTube. Maybe try reading a book instead. Hey, look at you! That's what you are choosing this minute. Good job.

SIT IN SILENCE

On a related note, when was the last time you sat alone, in silence, with nothing in your hands or in your ears?

French mathematician Blaise Pascal once said that "all of the unhappiness of men arises from one single fact, that they cannot stay quietly in their own chamber."[2] To which I feel like replying, "Blaise, you said that nearly four hundred years ago. You have no *idea* how bad things have gotten."

We're always on the go, it seems, always busily doing multiple things at once, constantly bombarding our minds with visuals and sound. Writer and consultant Linda Stone coined the phrase "continuous partial attention," which describes

> an always on, anywhere, anytime, any place behavior that creates an artificial sense of crisis. We are always in high alert. We are demanding multiple cognitively complex actions from ourselves. We are reaching to keep a top priority in focus, while, at the same time, scanning the periphery to see if we are missing other opportunities. If we are, our very fickle attention shifts focus. What's ringing? Who is it? How many emails? What's on my list? What time is it in Bangalore?[3]

EAT SMART AND DRINK WATER

I know some of this is so basic. But you cannot believe how much my mood changes based on what I eat and choose to drink and not drink. In the past year, as I have just simply changed what I eat and how much water I drink, my mental and emotional health has improved.

We wish all these little decisions didn't affect us so much. But we are mind, body, spiritual creatures, and each of those parts of us affects the other parts!

According to an editor at Harvard Health, "The inner workings of your digestive system don't just help you digest food, but also guide your emotions."[4] In fact, the balance of good and bad bacteria in our gut may have a direct effect on the serotonin our bodies produce to help regulate mood. All our favorite sugary treats and processed foods we eat to help us cope with stress may ultimately be making us feel worse!

Sigh.

Depressing, right?

It doesn't have to be. I know it's no fun to give up the foods we love, but unless those foods simultaneously love us back, they won't serve us well over time.

One of the things I've discovered on this journey is that way too many people are not depressed or anxious so much as they are simply dehydrated. This one is easy: You and I ought to be drinking water that is half our body weight in ounces per day.[5] If you weigh 150 pounds, you need seventy-five ounces of water each day. Easy, right?

MOVE AND GET OUTSIDE

There is no detriment to our health that is not vastly improved by exercise. Not a single one. Yet even before the pandemic and the shift to remote work, which, while easing stress in some ways, has resulted in us sitting for more hours in front of a screen, the average American adult was sitting for more than six hours a day.[6]

Honestly, I think we make exercise harder than it needs to be. If your question is, "What kind of exercise should I be doing?" the answer is this: "Whichever kind you'll actually do."

You have heard it before that the boost you get from exercise in your serotonin is similar to that of medicine. Whenever you feel like you are getting tangled up emotionally, take a walk. Do something that puts you back into your body. Jump in cold water. Run a sprint. Do a physical project. Whatever you do, try to get time outside if you can.

So much has been written on our present always-indoors situation that the term *"nature deficit disorder"* was coined to describe the impact of a lack of contact with the natural world. I see it even in my own life. There are plenty of days when I go from being inside my house to being inside my car to being inside my office to being inside a coffee shop or restaurant to being inside a grocery store to being back inside my house, and it's likely you could say the same of *your* normal, everyday life.

The dynamic is real.

Zac and I often walk in the evenings, and he read an article recently that blew both of our minds. It said that a "dose" equal to just twenty minutes per day, five days a week, of moderate-intensity physical activity (brisk walking, for example) reduces the risk of depressive symptoms and the chances of major depression. God made our bodies to move![7]

TAKE A NAP

Have you seen the little video out there with two toddler siblings? One of them is losing her ever-loving mind, and the other one looks at her and says, "Well, did you take your nap today?" And the first child, through her scream-crying, says, "Noooooooo." We aren't so different when we grow up.

Untangling emotions takes energy. Remember Charlie's five-hour midday nap? Give yourself some grace while you start working this process. If you're tired, then *go lie down.*

So many of our problems are solvable if we just make better choices to align our lives with our God-given limitations and adopt healthy practices. And then sometimes we are doing all that and still have found ourselves in a stronghold we just cannot get out of.

PAY FOR A FRIEND

In addition to all the choices we could make to better care for ourselves physically, I am convinced that the vast majority of us need one thing that, for whatever reason, we seem to resist: *a counselor.*

Yesterday my oldest, Conner, was in the backyard making the biggest mess with his truck. There was a tar-looking substance everywhere, including all over him, and his truck was jacked up.

When I asked what he was doing, he said, "I'm replacing my brakes."

Mmmhmmmm . . .

When I expressed my concern, he shot back, "Mom, I repair cars all the time."

True, my son has replaced tires and headlights, but replacing brakes? This felt, to me, like a big leap, like going from treading water in the peewee pool to trying to swim in the ocean.

A few hours later, I heard a crash, followed by my husband yelling.

Yeah, so the brakes weren't quite that simple.

Our neighbors are getting a new fence, and the eight-hundred-dollar repair charge my son was trying to avoid will end up cost-

ing him closer to five thousand to repair the damage to his truck
and the fence and to get the new brakes.

We do this with our emotional lives.

We think we are fine.

We think we don't need help.

We think we should be able to work it out ourselves.

If trauma and decades of hurt have accumulated, the situation
is way more serious than a quick tire change. It needs a professional. And that is okay. **You aren't especially broken; you are**
especially wise and strong to ask for help.

And doing so matters more than you can imagine.

My fears of abandonment are still there. I feel my chest get
tight at every appointment we attend for Zac's health. Today I can
name my fears and share them with him and others, and it eases.
But I don't know that I could have ever connected the dots all on
my own. From my seven-year-old self, afraid of death and equally
afraid of someone seeing my tears, to my early marriage when we
would fight and I couldn't breathe because my teammate had become my enemy and I felt completely alone, to Zac being in the
hospital, to our children growing up and a thousand other
moments—some too tender to share with you today—I don't
think I could have unwound that knot all on my own. I needed a
professional knot untangler to help me work through decades of
emotional twists.

Therapy isn't magic; we just all have a lot of tangled-up ropes.
Every one of us. What therapy does over long amounts of time,
depending on how tangled your ropes have become, is it helps
you pull on one little string and realize, dadgummit, everything is
more tangled up than you thought. For about six to eight weeks,
counseling just kind of ticks you off. You're not sure you want to

do it. But then, magically, a knot gets untangled. A moment that has haunted you for more than a decade starts to make sense and not haunt you but embolden you and define you in the best ways. At least that's about how it's always gone for me. I hate counseling until I love it.

Now, we nearly all have strings that, even when they're untangled, we'd still rather forget. We wish they weren't there. But when they're untangled, we can work with this thing. What was just a mangled mess of unusable Christmas lights in our garage becomes something beautiful and life giving and connected and has the hint and promise of connection between us and God and between us and the people we want to love well.

I hear well-meaning people say, "Look at the people who survived World War II. They are fine. They don't complain. We just need to get over it and pull ourselves up by our bootstraps and move on."

Many people who live like this are emotionally repressed! Yes, technically, people can make it through every kind of difficulty, even war. But in case you haven't noticed, we are in a full-on mental-health crisis in this country, and the situation is becoming even more dire. Spiritually and relationally and mentally, we're *still* paying the debts of unaddressed trauma from people around us shutting down emotionally and requiring that from the rest of us.

I want better for us and our kids.

May we be emotionally healthy, free, deeply connected to Jesus and each other.

You know by now, I'm a fan of therapy. I'm also aware that many people can't afford it. In its best, most ideal, realistic form, it comes regularly while we're doing life with the people we love.

I want to give you a little activity to help dinner dates and small groups try a little bit of healing therapy.

Text this to the people in your circle and ask that each of you share your answers next time you are together.

The biggest emotion I felt this week was _____.

The reason I felt _____ was _____. That feeling makes me feel_____, so I wanted to _____ the feeling.

I remember first feeling _____ when I was _____ years old. When I think about myself back then, it makes me feel _____.

I wish I could tell myself back then _____

_____.

NOT EASY, BUT WORTH IT

I want to shoot straight with you here before we wrap up this chapter. Despite my best suggestions and your best work, it is possible that you will be dealing with tangled-up emotions every day for the rest of your life.

I don't wish that for you.

I don't wish that for me.

Honestly, I don't *expect* it for either of us.

But it's possible, so I want to say it, plain as day.

Some people have been through so much that by the time they begin this work, the math on their healing just doesn't add up. Maybe the pile of stuff that has made your emotional load so large feels impossible to chip away at even if you had sixteen lifetimes.

Even so, what I know to be true is this: **We can be healthier than we are today. By God's grace, we can be transformed.** We can help the earlier versions of ourselves grow up a little and learn to exist in our newfound space. We can make strides. We can gain capacity. We can find peace where chaos reigned.

Yet, to be candid with you, I will tell you that such marvelous change will come at a cost. I have been moved to tears as I've watched friends and family members do the hard work of emotional healing. I've also been stunned by what that healing required.

I have seen friends and family members *radically change their lifestyle habits*. They've quit drinking. They've given up sugar. They've started doing yoga for the first time in their lives.

I've seen friends and family members *delete their social-media accounts*. I mean, *delete* delete. Not for Lent, but for good.

I've seen friends and family members who prefer a natural approach to well-being *gratefully start taking meds*. Zac is among this group. He doesn't want to be on psych drugs forever, I assure you. But he sees their validity for now.

I've seen friends and family members *adopt a brand-new friend group*. They needed friends who would support their progress instead of keeping them consigned to ill health, and—good for them—they went and found them. Man, the courage and drive this takes.

I've seen friends and family members *quit their jobs*. Their mental and emotional health was worth more than a big paycheck.

I've seen friends and family members *move to a different house, a different city, a different state.* No change is off-limits when your sanity is at stake!

I don't know what your emotional healing will demand of you, but it will, in fact, make demands. Will you come boldly to that discussion?

I hope you will.

I hope you always will.

I hope I'll do the same.

14

FREE TO FEEL

With the charge to write the final part of this book looming, I sat down yesterday morning at my favorite coffee shop once again to type away for you—and for two hours, no words came. I rarely have nothing to say. Writer's block hasn't been familiar to me in the many years and projects I've created. But with the pressure growing, my chest began to get tight. My heart rate began to increase. I couldn't sit still. I tried to push through, but eventually, with only one sentence written, I stood up, paid, and left.

I got in my car and drove aimlessly. I just couldn't think of what to do or even where to go. I ended up in my driveway, just camped out in my car with my fear growing to near panic.

Frankly, so many other pressures were right behind the writing deadline pressing in on me. A kid struggling in school, my husband far from home for work, my sister's son in the hospital once again. The list really could just go on and on and on.

Do you relate? Like everything just feels so out of control and broken? I know, I know. It is. The irony is not lost on me that I can't finish my book about feelings because of my overwhelming feelings.

The nausea-inducing pressure and feelings didn't go away,

even as I later picked up my son from school and prepared to host our evening small group at my house. I didn't really want the group to come over; I wanted to put on my robe, crawl into bed early, and watch another mind-numbing show.

But they came. Surrounded by some of my most safe people, men and women we have done deep life with for years, I participated in the discussion, answering the questions posed for the night:

How has the past year changed you?

How do you need God to show up for you in the next three months?

Early in this book, I told you that I am different from when I started this journey. I've learned that emotions aren't the enemy. Emotions are the gift. Emotions are meant to pull us in to God and each other. Because of that, where I would have normally postured a simple vague answer to where I need God to show up for me, instead I broke down with these people who love me.

I told them the pressures I feel.

The anxiety leading me to spend a lot of the day in the car alone, not knowing what to do. . . .

The fear that these words will never be enough to actually help people. . . .

The deep longing to be better than I am at this enormous job God has called me to. . . .

I even shared the embarrassing part that lately I have found myself jealous of other people who seem to be so much better than me at the jobs I am called to do.

I said all that while I awkwardly looked at the ground, with tears falling to the floor and wondering the whole time if I was being too emotional for the men in the room.

But guess what?

They hugged me. They listened. Then they shared their hard. All the women and all the men. Each one sharing their feelings and struggles.

It was so beautiful and simple and real and awkward and hopeful.

And at the end, Ashley, my sister-in-law turned best friend, leaned over and said, "I feel better. Do you?"

I did. I actually did.

And now this morning, I don't have writer's block. I have a vision for you. For us.

I picture you free. Free to feel. Free to share those feelings, and free to run into God's presence with it all. Going from all knotted and tangled up to the adventurous life God has for you full of joy, fear, anger, sadness—all of it!

It makes me think of the time Zac thought it would be a good idea to strap all of us into harnesses and do a ridiculously long zip line.

As I snapped on my helmet and climbed the massive steel platform, I glanced up at Zac, who was leading our offspring. I'd feed off his confidence while I got my bearings. This was totally safe, right? Nothing to fear, right?

Moments later, I watched as my husband, followed by my eldest son and then each of the other kids, hopped from the metal launch platform and soared over the treetops and out of my line of sight like there was nothing to it. And then it was my turn. As I scooted from safety and felt gravity start to whirl the sheave over the cable, I laughed aloud.

I cruised along that mile-long cable at upward of thirty miles per hour for only a handful of minutes, but the realization I made while I was up there has stayed with me ever since: Soaring is a heck of a lot more fun than staying stuck. It's true on a zip line, and it's true in everyday life.

Living with impossibly tangled-up feelings is about as satisfying as riding on a zip line with knots. Sure, you could thrust and jerk your way down the line to the platform at the bottom and technically say that you'd taken the ride, but wouldn't you have missed the whole point of the thing? Wouldn't you want a refund?

In the same way, **living life tangled up emotionally is not really living at all.** What I've been learning the past two or three years is that you and I were made not to stagger our way through this earthly experience, but instead to soar. Really. Not because life is always easy. It's not. But because despite the challenges, it's possible to keep moving, to keep growing, to keep being awestruck over the ride.

GETTING UNSTUCK

During the time I have worked on this book, Zac has emerged from those months of depression and is in a completely different place today.

He made it through another valley, and he came out the other side. I watched him live this book as I wrote it. He cried when he needed to cry, he shared everything with his closest people, and he wasn't afraid to face all his sadness and feel it.

We walk often at night.

For months on our walks, Zac was quiet, and then some nights he told me all the unfair parts that were making him just flat furi-

ous, and other nights it was worry about our future, and sometimes it was sadness that in some way he had let us down.

Somewhere as these words were being written, our walks became happier. Nothing had changed in our circumstances, but he
got lighter and more hopeful and peaceful again. There were even
some nights he laughed.

I've learned that I want to be in for the walks together, whatever they hold. On the very best nights and the very worst. We
can be in that fully, wholeheartedly together.

Circumstances turned, but not before he did.

Zac's business came back from the brink of death and is going
to work. Today Kate and Charlie live not too far away, but even
this week the conversation of a potential move came up and my
heart didn't stop; my chest didn't get tight. In fact, it was a fun
conversation to dream of what could be for them. The circumstances of our lives feel more peaceful, but I've learned to relish it
all at the same time—from the tears on the floor with my middle
school son to the joy of a wedding and beginning of a new family.
I've learned it all is so rich and good, and I don't want to miss any
of it.

All the feelings with all our people.

Zac tells me that he never once felt alone, even when his depression was at its worst. This was because people who had been where
he now was came alongside him and refused to let him drown.
Their sheer presence told him day by day that despite how crappy
he felt, despite how unknowable he seemed to himself, things
would get better over time. He would make it to the other side.

This is, incidentally, part of the reason I was determined to
write this book, so that you or anyone else who was scraping by
emotionally might find encouragement to stay the course. Even

the most stuck person can get unstuck. Zac and I both are living proof of that fact. My goal is that should you ever feel stuck, you will come to believe that too.

THE GIFTS OF EMOTIONAL HEALTH

Eugene Peterson wrote so beautifully that "the aim of the person of faith is . . . to live as deeply and thoroughly as possible—to deal with the reality of life, discover truth, create beauty, act out love."[1]

Yes. This is living. This is the redemptive work of God through us on earth. To feel it all, to notice it and name it and issue the hope of God to a desperate world.

I wanted to name this book *Ten Thousand Dollars' Worth of Counseling*—ha! Because I tried my best to do something impossible. To help you feel seen, to help you navigate the vast wild ocean of your emotions, to reconnect you to your people and God as you do it. Lofty goals and a very lofty subject. I hope it has at least felt like a little bit of help on your way.

As we come to the end of this journey, I am so aware that these words are limited, that I can't help you live perfectly emotionally healthy and free. God can and will over time. He's working it all out in those of us who follow Him. But as we go, I want to leave you with a few gifts to notice as you grow in emotional health.

GIFT #1: WE HAVE HOPE AGAIN

A few nights ago, one of my best friends, Emily, and I were at dinner. She sat down and without any small talk launched right in. "I'm afraid I am depressed." Emily is in a lot of counseling right now, working though decades of hard junk, digging it all up. She said, "It feels like everything is getting worse, not better— yet."

Yet. She still had hope it would turn. It was a tiny sliver, but today, even as I write these words, she is at her counselor's office for her next session because, as hopeless as some circumstances feel, she chooses to hope enough to show up and give God room to work.

Resilience and perseverance require hope. We would all stay in our beds permanently if it weren't for hope. We believe, even if it's just a small little sliver, that things could possibly be better than they are.

The Enemy's goal for you is hopelessness.

To quit hoping that your child will be healed from their eating disorder.

To quit hoping that your marriage will ever get easier.

To quit hoping that your depression or anxiety will ever get better.

To quit hoping in the people around you to be safe places, so you never share.

To quit hoping that God could ever help all the wrongs in your life make sense.

To quit hoping that healing is possible.

This is his great scheme and plan, and he'll use any tactic to take hope from you.

You know what makes me so sad? You might feel helpless. Hopeless. Yet if you know Jesus, you are filled with the Holy Spirit, the greatest supernatural helper of all time. Better than any super-hero ever. He contains all knowledge and power. He is yours in

Christ Jesus. **You are never helpless.** As I invite you to feel your feelings, remember that they don't have authority over you; rather, you have authority over them because of Christ Jesus.

In this world, we have trouble. Fact.

And Jesus has overcome the world. Fact.

GIFT #2: WE GROW IN GRACE TOWARD OURSELVES AND OTHERS

In college, I was deeply influenced by the writings of the late theologian Brennan Manning. His most famous work is titled *The Ragamuffin Gospel,* but every single book in his backlist is worth your time. He's that good. Yet for all his writing prowess and kingdom impact—I'm talking millions upon millions of books sold—Brennan struggled with the demons of addiction until the day he died.

People would ask Brennan how it was possible that he could love Jesus as much as he said he did while still choosing to drink until he passed out drunk with some degree of frequency. How could he be so attached to Jesus while remaining addicted to alcohol? Weren't these two things mutually exclusive? Shouldn't he have to pick?

I bet he wished he could pick.

In response to questions and assumptions and allegations along these lines, Brennan had a phrase he would always say. It wasn't said pridefully or sarcastically or rudely; it was said from a place of humility. "These things happen," he would say.

These things happen, indeed.

Life is complex. It is messy. It is marked by confusion and curiosity and pain. On way too many occasions, we identify less with Jesus's call to perfect holiness than we do with the apostle Paul's lament over doing what he didn't want to do and not doing what he did want to do.[2] At times, it's enough to make us want to give up. To detach. To lose hope.

What Brennan's reply means to me is that given the choice between utter hopelessness and concession that things here on planet Earth aren't exactly as we wish them to be, then I, too, would pick concession. "These things happen" would be *my* play too.

In the same way, "These things happen" is a way of acknowledging that although this lovely lunacy we call life is absolutely imperfect, don't we still long to live it? Don't we still try to fly?

In describing my journey toward emotional wellness, *imperfect* would be a fair word to use.

About a year ago, I stopped by a gathering and happened to hear one friend saying to another friend something negative that seemed to be about me, which caught me off guard. There was so much busyness going on in that place that I was able to kind of blend into the situation without her knowing that I'd heard what she'd said, but as soon as I could make a graceful exit, I beelined it for home and retreated to my room.

I was devastated. How could she do this to me?

The whole ordeal stung deeply, and I wasn't sure what to do. But doing nothing wasn't an option; she and I are tight. We're committed to being in community together.

Several days later, once my emotional tailspin had slowed, I called my friend. She picked up. I said, "Hey." And then as calmly as I could, I told her that I'd heard what she'd said about me at the party. And that I felt very misunderstood. And that I thought our friendship was a safe place for me to be. And that I'd trusted her before but now just wasn't sure.

She was silent for a beat and then said, "I'm so sorry, Jennie. You're right."

In a calm, tender tone, my friend then confided in me a situation from her life story I hadn't yet heard. Through a swirl of thoughts and emotions coursing through my mind and heart, I got off that call thinking, *I get why she said what she said, and we're going to be okay.*

For sure, there were some awkward moments after that whole ordeal. She felt bad. I felt judged. It took us a minute to feel safe again. But we recovered, and it actually deepened our friendship, because these things happen. They do.

My point: This work is going to put you in awkward situations, but the awkward gets better over time.

I want to encourage you that as you start acknowledging how you are truly feeling and you start sharing those feelings with other living, breathing human beings, the weird stuff you will encounter will seem like it has no bounds. Someone will misspeak. Someone will misunderstand. Someone will take offense. Someone will overshare. Someone will spread a confidential update. On and on it goes. But if your experience is anything like mine, over time the weird will start to normalize. Things get better as you go.

And until the dynamic settles down a little, I try to keep two things in mind: First, I don't need the people I'm sharing with to be perfect at every turn. Can you imagine if that were my standard? I would fail my own impossible test!

We are broken people living in a broken world, every last one of us. To expect flawed individuals to somehow be flawless is a me problem, not a problem with them.

So, that's the first thing. The second one is this: I screw up so often too.

I can say the wrong thing and do. I can misunderstand and do. I can be easily offended. I can ridiculously overshare. And because I can get things so wrong, I can quickly forgive others when they do the same.

This stuff is awkward! You know what? It's also worth it. We were made for community. We are messy and imperfect, and we get to be. Because of the grace of God for us.

GIFT #3: WE GET GOD

As you're growing in wholeheartedness and health, increasingly and seemingly without having to *will* it, you'll start bringing your feelings to Jesus before trying to make sense of them on your own.

The truth about dealing with our feelings is that if we don't take them to God, they will likely overtake us. They don't have to overtake us.

I posted an Instagram survey where I asked people how they felt about their feelings and what kept them from the emotional health we all seem to desire. One of the biggest topics that surfaced was whether our emotions are somehow sinful or wrong.

- Are you sure it's okay to feel my emotions? Doesn't this make me an irresponsible Christian or someone who lacks true faith in God?

- How can I unlearn that some feelings are bad/shameful/ evil? This was the messaging I received in the church.

- What's the line between experiencing anger and sinning because of it? Or experiencing any emotion and sinning because of it, for that matter?

We ask these questions—and others like them—only if we somehow stop believing that God fashioned us into the people we are today, complete with a wide emotional range. It is absolutely not irresponsible to feel our emotions fully, if those emotions have been surrendered to God. There is absolutely no such thing as a negative emotion, if we are careful to surrender every emotion to God. We absolutely do not need to fear acting in an inappropriate manner if as soon as we experience the emotion, we turn toward God and say, "Please help."

Far better to regard our emotions as the gifts they are instead of stuffing them so they can't make us sin. We are not our emotions. Our emotions don't last forever. **God longs to use our emotions to help us become better at living this thing called life.**

You'll recall that when I first started meeting with my cohort and Dr. C, I told the group that the frustration and anger that seemed to be overtaking me were due to feeling set adrift by God. I had felt set up by Him and then abandoned, and it stung worse than I can describe. But just as the disciples who were in the boat with Jesus one time when a storm erupted at sea needed to learn, those storms we face with God draw us into deeper intimacy with Him.

God hadn't set me adrift.

God hadn't abandoned me.

God had allowed the waves to pick up and the winds to blow so that I would bury my face in Him.

What God is after in your life and mine is relationship.

It's proximity.

It's intimacy.

It's peace.

He wants you.

He wants me.

He wants us to find our relief in Him.

We're okay, the disciples finally realized, after they took their fear to Jesus instead.

We're okay. We're okay. Everything will be just fine.

That outcome can be true for us too. God doesn't ask us to stop being afraid or concerned or frustrated or angry or sad; He simply asks us to stick close to His side:

> Whoever dwells in the shelter of the Most High
>> will rest in the shadow of the Almighty.
> I will say of the LORD, "He is my refuge and my fortress,
>> my God, in whom I trust."
> Surely he will save you
>> from the fowler's snare
>> and from the deadly pestilence.
> He will cover you with his feathers,
>> and under his wings you will find refuge;
>> his faithfulness will be your shield and rampart.[3]

We really are under His wings, all tucked in, safe and sound. And in that place of refuge, we can feel anything we need to feel.

GIFT #4: WE CONTROL WHAT WE CAN, AND WE STOP TRYING TO CONTROL THE THINGS WE CAN'T

Today, as I look back at the impact and pages of my book *Get Out of Your Head,* I'm struck by how absolutely crucial the words of this current book are to those earlier insights.

Yes, we have control over our thoughts, but life is never that clean and simple. Before you have a thought, you have a feeling, an abstract sense that something is wrong or right, and that feeling can't be wished or prayed away. It must come up to the surface and be faced, seen, soothed, made to feel safe. And as that happens, we heal. And our thoughts change too.

We have dominion and God-given authority over our minds—yes, it's true! If you haven't read *Get Out of Your Head* yet, I hope you'll go get it. I meant these two books to complement one another. They are both so true and yet so different, because we are complex creatures built by an impossible-to-get-our-head-around God.

I just heard a friend mention the Serenity Prayer, spoken at the beginning of every Alcoholics Anonymous meeting. I think it so perfectly applies here:

> God, grant me the serenity to accept the things
>   I cannot change,
> The courage to change the things I can,
> And the wisdom to know the difference.[4]

Some of life we can control, and so much of it we cannot.

Some thoughts we can interrupt, and some feelings will not go away no matter what it seems we do. And God wants to be in all of it with us. In the boat on the ocean, navigating it all.

GIFT #5: WE START CREATING AGAIN

In Ecclesiastes, King Solomon, who was considered the wisest man ever to live, wrote this:

For everything there is a season, and a time for every matter under heaven:

a time to be born, and a time to die;
a time to plant, and a time to pluck up what is planted;
a time to kill, and a time to heal;
a time to break down, and a time to build up;
a time to weep, and a time to laugh;
a time to mourn, and a time to dance;
a time to cast away stones, and a time to gather stones
   together;
a time to embrace, and a time to refrain from embracing;
a time to seek, and a time to lose;
a time to keep, and a time to cast away;
a time to tear, and a time to sew;
a time to keep silence, and a time to speak;
a time to love, and a time to hate;
a time for war, and a time for peace.[5]

There is supposed to be a rhythm to life, this passage is saying.
We are supposed to experience ups as well as downs. We should
expect seasons to our existence. Things aren't intended to stay the
same. Life follows death follows life. There is uprooting to balance
the planting. Yes, we mourn, but we'll dance again.

My counselor, Dr. C (aka Dr. Curt Thompson), has a hypoth-
esis that I love. He says that one of the ways to tell that we're starting to make progress in our emotional healing is that we will start
creating again.[6] When we're stuck in a cycle of judging and fighting back our emotions—controlling them, turning to coping mechanisms, or concealing them to try to get by—all our energy gets
used up in the process, and we have no energy left to *live, to create.*

The moment we learn how to feel our feelings and not run from them or judge them, we free up all that energy we were pouring into *not feeling* them all those years. We're then able to live life as it was meant to be lived, complete with highs and lows and joy and grief and mourning and dancing and love and sometimes loss. We get all the shades of existence where only gray used to exist. What's more: All that energy we were wasting is finally available for us to contribute something beautiful to the world.

Last summer, God gave me a vision that felt way too big for me. It was a vision to host a gathering for His glory involving people from all over the world. Interestingly, if this vision had come to me two years earlier, given how emotionally unhealthy I was, I probably would have scoffed. I would have said no. *You want me to do what? Yeah, no, not going to happen.* Too much pressure. Too big a burden. Too likely I would fail.

But that's not when He gave me this vision.

He gave it to me as I started to heal.

As we make our way toward emotional wellness, we have increased capacity to *serve.* As we make our way toward emotional wellness, we have increased capacity to *give.* As we make our way toward emotional wellness, we have increased capacity to *care.*

God knew I had room to care, so He issued an invitation to create.

I sat in a room for eight full hours yesterday with a team of people God has rallied around this particular vision, and do you know how I felt as I drove home after such a long day?

Energized.

Excited.

Ready to go.

How is that possible? Eight hours? Wrestling over super-complex topics? Doing something that feels too big to do?

Yep: ready to go. *Come on, God. Bring it on.*

God wants to go wild through us, for us, but if we ignore or get tangled in the ropes meant to bring Him and others close to us, we are missing all of it: the creating, the loving, the peace, the connection, the hope, the very best parts of our short life here.

We will be made whole and free and well in heaven. That promise is coming for those who trust Jesus. But I want that now. I want that wholeness and freedom for us here if it is ours to have. And it is.

15

YOUR FEELINGS ARE
WORTH FIGHTING FOR

There is no hard-and-fast formula for untangling our emotions. But there is progress we can make, and the gifts of emotional health I described in the preceding chapter can assure us that we're on the right path. It's a path worth following, I promise you. It's the path that leads to wholeheartedness, to emotional sturdiness, to peace.

Not long ago, I was reflecting on the journey I've been on, this big, bold transformation from being Fix-It Jennie to Feel-It Jennie. I wouldn't say I've arrived, if arrival is even a possibility, but I've definitely made my way so far up the path that there is no way I'd turn back now.

In our family of six, my daughter Kate has always been our big feeler, by far our most emotional child. For as long as I can remember, whereas most people have a heart, Kate's heart has always had her. She has always felt everyone's pain. She has always entered into everyone's joy. She has always fallen in love so easily, determined to believe the best—always the best. And while this may sound like a beautiful way to live, I was always worried for her. Wouldn't she get hurt or offended or wounded or wronged somehow?

On way too many occasions, I would come to Kate with tool belt on, eager to repair whatever was broken in her world. And every time, without exception, she would look at me and say, "Don't fix me, Mom."

Can you think of anything worse than to tell a lifelong fixer that you *didn't* want fixing from them? I felt devastated every time. *But fixing is what I'm good at! Maybe the only thing I do well.*

I wanted to be the mom Kate needed—I truly did. I just didn't have any of the right gear.

Several months ago, I was sitting across from Kate, listening to her explain a deep source of sorrow in her life. She was crying as she searched for the right words to say. My baby, now married, was sad. And in that moment, it's like all of a sudden I could see the experience in split screen. On one side was Kate working through this terribly broken thing, and on the other side was my realization that I had no desire to fix it. I was just sitting there. Fully present. Bearing witness to her emotion. Being a safe place for my girl.

In quiet moments, I can slip into that awful place where I kick myself for getting it wrong all those years. *Why couldn't I have been what Kate had needed before? Why did it take me so long to learn it?*

Let me tell you what catches me every time I wonder things like this: I could have been the world's most perfect mom to Kate and still couldn't have met every last one of her emotional needs. What she needed, only Jesus could provide. And thankfully, she turned to Him.

Zac turned to Him too. As I finish this book today, many of the things that fell apart at the beginning are restored. He is healthy and laughing and full of all the things that make him Zac. Before his company was okay, he was okay. He's learned the art of noticing, naming, feeling, and sharing the sadness and the joy. I'm still learning, so my heart can't help but feel relieved that we're in a season of joy.

AT SMALL GROUP recently, my pastor friend said a phrase I've heard many times: "I just want to fight for joy." It struck me in a new way that maybe that's what I want for myself and for you with this book. Or maybe that's what I started off wanting for you.

But as everyone shared their fears and griefs and disappointments and anger last night, I found myself happy for it all. I even pushed back and said, "I'm glad to have friends who fight for sadness and anger and fear too, because somehow hope feels more real in the midst of those things than on the days everything goes right and we're full of joy."

If I look back at my life and think of my deepest experiences with God, they aren't on the days I felt joy. They are on the days when I couldn't get out of my car because of fear, when I couldn't show up at work because of tears, when I couldn't even speak because I was so mad.

Yeah, let's fight for joy, because we have
a lot to be joyful for
a lot to be hopeful for
a lot to be grateful for.

But let's surprise the world and also be sad and angry and scared when it is fitting—not because our God isn't big enough to conquer those things, but because He's big enough to hold those things. Our faith is big enough to hope in the midst of those things.

He built us with the capacity to carry joy, sadness, fear, anger, and more all at the same time. Part of me yesterday was afraid the words of this book wouldn't be significant enough to change anything, and part of me couldn't believe I got to build these words for you. My job is to be your encourager and point you to Jesus.

I can have both joy and fear coexisting in my body about the same circumstance at the exact same time. Maybe this is why the whole world feels depressed and anxious today. We forgot that we can contain fear and joy, sadness and hope at the same moment. As I look ahead at Zac's and my life, part of me is afraid of all we still have to face, from work to kids to personal struggles, so much of it out of our control, and part of me can't wait to see what God has in store. That is how it's supposed to go.

For so long, I just didn't know it.

The new me isn't afraid of emotions. I expect them. They come wave upon wave, sometimes because of a circumstance and sometimes because of my mood. Sometimes just because I'm human. Today I let those feelings come. I notice them. I form a word around what they are. I let them seep down into all the parts of me because I can be sad and not fall into the dark pit I've feared all my life. And if the feelings are significant enough, I can tell someone. If the valley lasts long enough, I decide what I should do about it.

This process isn't as organized as I've made it sound. It's the messiest part of life. It's the least likely thing to be controlled. Even with many of my emotions untangled, they're still waving in the wind, begging for someone to pick up the other side of the rope and make sense of it all.

But the maturity of where I am today is that I don't need to make sense of it all. And I do not need to judge it. I can live in the tension of pain and happiness all in a given hour. I can laugh and cry all in a given hour. And all of that equals a full life that I wouldn't want to miss.

I feel again. Doing so has given me my greatest friendships and conversations and led to my greatest hope, which is for that future day when every tear will be dried and every wrong will be made right. Every pain will be healed for eternity because our ultimate connection will be fulfilled with God and with each other if we know Him.

One day we'll understand it all. We'll see it all as He sees it. In the meantime, we get God and each other and a chance to live this one life with hearts whole, living, beating, feeling, full, connected to God and to each other. That is the life I want.

That is the life He wants for you.

ACKNOWLEDGMENTS

This was the most difficult book I have ever written. So many tensions to hold! And I knew every single one of you who would pick it up is coming into this conversation in a different place. Zac says it is my bravest book. And it did feel that way.

I've learned the secret in life: Never do anything alone. The scarier something is, the more people you need around you. I had an army.

First, to the people who this book is dedicated to and the ones I do everyday life with: You let me feel my way to my own feelings awkwardly and with so much patience. My friends laugh because almost daily as I was writing, I would use the words *"I feel . . ."* And many of those days, the feeling was *sad* or *overwhelmed* or *scared.* And you stuck with me and listened and prayed and even felt it with me on the worst days.

Thank you for being the safe people to share with—Ashley, Lindsey, Jennie E., Julie, Meg, Kat A., Carla, Michelle, Ellen, Liz, Kat M., Jess, Melissa, Toni, Jamie, Ann, Callie, and more! Thank you for being safe and for caring (at times more than I do) about this work!

Second, Zac Allen: You take over for months and months while I am single-mindedly consumed with this work. And you insisted I share your story here, knowing it would help many people and hopefully many men find emotional health. Your zeal for wholeheartedness has been my example on my journey. Thank you.

To my kids: You always cheer me on in ways I don't deserve

because this work takes me away from you at times. You never complain; you cheer! You care. You want to know about it. You want to read it. It means the world to me. Conner, Kate, Charlie, Caroline, and Coop: You know you are my favorite part of life. You are it, and I want to be emotionally healthy for you! I pray I am a safe place for all your feelings and seasons. I love you.

My family: Mom and Dad, thank you for being so steady. I have always felt safe with you, and you loved us well and provided a secure, loving home for me, Brooke, and Katie to flourish. You were doting, generous parents! I am so grateful. And, Carolyn and Randy, you built my two favorite humans on earth! Zac is the most incredible man because of you, and Ashley is my best friend! Well done, all four of you, at loving us well!

Chloe, we have had a ride these past ten years. I know none of this work would be what it is without your help behind the scenes. You are the greatest teammate and friend! Thank you for being calm when I freak out. Thank you for keeping all the plates in the air spinning when I check out for months to create. Thank you for pool days, helping me research and reading and editing every word. Thank you for your creativity that shapes all my work!

Emily, Terri, Molly, and Julia: You keep it all going and make sending my work into the world so fun! Thanks for being on this team and committed to seeing this help people.

Thank you, Shae and Lysa, for always dreaming with me and making my work better! You are so ridiculously generous!

Parker, whenever writing alone just became too much, I would call you and you would stop whatever you were doing and type my words for a while just so I didn't have to be alone. You made the months of this doable. Thank you for always showing up for me for all the boring stuff. I can't believe you keep saying yes to my crazy!

My IF:Gathering team, this year has required more faith and work than any before it! You have carried a weighty vision while I have been away writing. I am so sorry for the pressure that my absence puts on you. Yet you celebrate my writing, show up to brainstorm with me, and support me in ways I couldn't have dreamed of! Brooke, Bonner, Cheryl, Luke, Hannah M., Amy Bay, Lisa, Jordyn, Hannah B., Hannah R., Caroline (Parker) B., Jessie, Kaley G., Greer, Callie, Halee, Elizabeth, Amanda, Meg, Kayley M., Aly, Traci, Katy, Kristen, Merich, new and old team—you made this possible. Thank you! And for all that is coming, it is going to be epic! Let's go!

The Yates and Yates team, thank you for taking a risk on me! Sometimes I feel happier for our wins for you than for me. Because you took such a risk, I am always so relieved it proved worthwhile. Thank you for showing me appreciation and stopping to celebrate with me. I am so grateful for ten years together! Curtis and Karen, you are family to us. And I cannot imagine if we hadn't met so many years ago. Our lives would not be the same.

WaterBrook, our relationship has been so helpful to my work! You have believed in me more than I have believed in myself. You have said a thousand yeses that helped our work together reach the whole world! Thank you for how much you care about this! I could not ask for a better team: Tina, Campbell, Bev, Ginia, Jo, Elizabeth, Laura W., Todd, Lori, and so many more.

And finally, to Ashley Wiersma and Laura Barker, this book would not exist or be helpful at all without your love and commitment to it! Ashley, your help with research and creativity made me believe this was a good idea, and you helped it exist! I love that we are so different and honest with each other. It makes the work better! And, Laura, you lose sleep and fight to get it all right. You are the best editor I have ever worked with!

Even though this project involved hundreds of hours of me alone writing, I knew I was not really alone. Thank you for taking my crazy calls and for caring as much as I do that this be all God wants it to be!

NOTES

CHAPTER 1: WHERE DID *THAT* COME FROM?

1. Mary West, "What Is the Fight, Flight, or Freeze Response?," *Medical News Today,* July 29, 2021, www.medicalnewstoday .com/articles/fight-flight-or-freeze-response.

CHAPTER 2: ALL TANGLED UP

1. Jonathan Edwards, *Jonathan Edwards' Resolutions: And Advice to Young Converts,* ed. Stephen J. Nichols (Phillipsburg, N.J.: P&R Publishing, 2001), 17.
2. "What Makes Memories Stronger?," The University of Queensland, https://qbi.uq.edu.au/brain-basics/memory/ what-makes-memories-stronger.
3. Peter Scazzero, *Emotionally Healthy Spirituality: It's Impossible to Be Spiritually Mature While Remaining Emotionally Immature* (Grand Rapids, Mich.: Zondervan, 2017), 44.
4. Robert Osserman, "Knot Theory," *Encyclopaedia Britannica,* May 17, 2016, www.britannica.com/science/knot-theory.

CHAPTER 3: WHERE DID THE MESS BEGIN?

1. I first referenced this concept in my book *Find Your People:* Tina Payne Bryson, PhD, "When Children Feel Safe, Seen, and Soothed (Most of the Time), They Develop Security," January 9, 2020, www.tinabryson.com/news/when-children

-feel-safe-seen-amp-soothed-most-of-the-time-they-develop
-security.

2. Lindsay C. Gibson, *Adult Children of Emotionally Immature Parents: How to Heal from Distant, Rejecting, or Self-
Involved Parents* (Oakland, Calif.: New Harbinger, 2015), 164.

3. Jeremiah 17:9.

4. I found this resource helpful in my research: J. Alasdair
Groves and Winston T. Smith, *Untangling Emotions*
(Wheaton, Ill.: Crossway, 2019).

5. *Oxford English Dictionary*, s.v. "asceticism (*n.*)," www.oed
.com/search/dictionary/?scope=Entries&q=asceticism.

CHAPTER 4: THE TRUTH ABOUT YOUR FEELINGS

1. Jill Seladi-Schulman, "What Part of the Brain Controls
Emotions?," Healthline, July 24, 2018, www.healthline
.com/health/what-part-of-the-brain-controls-emotions.

2. Adam Hoffman, "Can Negative Thinking Make You Sick?,"
Health, January 4, 2023, www.health.com/condition/heart
-disease/can-negative-thinking-make-you-sick.

3. Therese J. Borchard, "7 Good Reasons to Cry: The Healing
Property of Tears," PsychCentral, May 29, 2011, https://
psychcentral.com/blog/7-good-reasons-to-cry-the-healing
-property-of-tears#1.

4. "Exercise: 7 Benefits of Regular Physical Activity," Mayo
Clinic, October 8, 2021, www.mayoclinic.org/healthy
-lifestyle/fitness/in-depth/exercise/art-20048389.

5. 2 Peter 3:9.

6. Isaiah 53:3.

7. See Luke 22:41–44.

8. See Isaiah 63:10; Ephesians 4:30.

9. See James 4:4–5.

10. See Romans 8:26.

11. Hebrews 4:15, KJV, emphasis added.

12. Ephesians 4:26.

13. See Matthew 5:28.

14. See Romans 6.

CHAPTER 5: EXPERTS IN EVASIVE MEASURES

1. "GeneSight Mental Health Monitor: Addictive Behaviors," GeneSight, https://genesight.com/mental-health-monitor/addictive-behaviors.

CHAPTER 6: CREATED TO CONNECT

1. John 8:31–32, 36.

2. See 1 Corinthians 2:9–11.

3. Exodus 3:14.

4. Matthew 18:3, NIV.

5. Matthew 5:4.

6. Hebrews 4:15–16.

7. Luke 4:18–19, NIV.

8. Psalm 51:6, NASB.

9. Genesis 2:18.

10. Curt Thompson, *Anatomy of the Soul: Surprising Connections Between Neuroscience and Spiritual Practices That Can Transform Your Life and Relationships* (Carol Stream, Ill.: Tyndale, 2010), 99.

CHAPTER 7: A VISION FOR SOMETHING BETTER

1. See Deuteronomy 31:8.

CHAPTER 8: GETTING PAST *FINE*

1. Sanjay Srivastava et al., "The Social Costs of Emotional Suppression: A Prospective Study of the Transition to College," *Journal of Personality and Social Psychology* 96, no. 4 (2009), 883–97, https://doi.org/10.1037/a0014755.
2. Lucy Cousins, "Can Always Staying Positive Be Bad for Our Health?," The Hospitals Contribution Fund of Australia Limited, August 2022, www.hcf.com.au/health-agenda/body-mind/mental-health/downsides-to-always-being-positive.
3. Select concepts in this chapter are distilled and adapted from Lisa Feldman Barrett, *How Emotions Are Made: The Secret Life of the Brain* (New York: Mariner, 2017).
4. Mark 5:34.
5. Mary C. Lamia, "Getting Things Done, Procrastinating or Not," *Psychology Today*, March 8, 2017, www.psychologytoday.com/us/blog/intense-emotions-and-strong-feelings/201703/getting-things-done-procrastinating-or-not.

CHAPTER 9: THE VOCABULARY OF EMOTION

1. 2 Corinthians 4:8, NIV.
2. Daniel J. Siegel and Tina Payne Bryson, *The Whole-Brain*

Child: 12 Revolutionary Strategies to Nurture Your Child's Developing Mind (New York: Bantam, 2012), 27.

3. See John 1:38; Matthew 8:26; 14:31; 20:32; John 21:17.

4. My approach to the Big Four emotions is partially based on my research into the work of clinical psychologist and researcher Dr. Paul Ekman. More information on his work and insights can be found at www.PaulEkman.com.

5. See John 10:10.

6. See John 10:10.

7. John 15:11.

8. James 1:19.

9. Exodus 34:6.

10. See Ephesians 4:26.

11. Ephesians 4:26, NIV.

12. Joseph P. Forgas, "Four Ways Sadness May Be Good for You," *Greater Good Magazine,* June 4, 2014, https://greatergood.berkeley.edu/article/item/four_ways_sadness_may_be_good_for_you.

13. 1 Samuel 13:14.

14. Isaiah 41:10; Jeremiah 1:8; Matthew 14:27; 10:31, NIV; Luke 12:32; John 14:27, NIV.

15. For a fascinating read on this subject, you might check out Lisa Feldman Barrett's book *How Emotions Are Made: The Secret Life of the Brain* (New York: Mariner, 2017).

16. Todd B. Kashdan, Lisa Feldman Barrett, and Patrick E. McKnight, "Unpacking Emotion Differentiation: Transforming Unpleasant Experience by Perceiving Distinctions in Negativity," *Current Directions in Psychological Science* 24, no. 1 (2015), 10–16, https://doi.org/10.1177/0963721414550708.

CHAPTER 10: GIVE YOURSELF SOME SPACE

1. James 1:2–4.
2. Gabor Maté, *When the Body Says No: Exploring the Stress-Disease Connection* (Hoboken, N.J.: Wiley, 2003), 166.
3. Brett Ford, quoted in Marianna Pogosyan, "Can Emotions Be Controlled?," *Psychology Today,* November 27, 2018, www.psychologytoday.com/us/blog/between-cultures/201811/can-emotions-be-controlled.
4. David P. Murray, *Christians Get Depressed Too: Hope and Help for Depressed People* (Grand Rapids, Mich.: Reformation Heritage, 2010).

CHAPTER 11: YOU ARE NOT ALONE IN THIS

1. Guy Vingerhoets, "Our Emotional Brains: Both Sides Process the Language of Feelings, with the Left Side Labeling the 'What' and the Right Side Processing the 'How,'" American Psychological Association, 2003, www.apa.org/news/press/releases/2003/01/emotional-brains.
2. Galatians 6:2.
3. Matthew 11:30.
4. See John 16:33, NIV, and Matthew 16:24.
5. John 11:21.
6. John 11:25–26.
7. See John 11:33–35.
8. Romans 12:15, NIV.
9. Romans 5:3–5, NKJV.

CHAPTER 12: WHAT TO DO WITH WHAT YOU FEEL

1. 1 Peter 5:7, NIV.
2. "U.S. Teen Girls Experiencing Increased Sadness and Violence," Centers for Disease Control and Prevention, February 13, 2023, www.cdc.gov/media/releases/2023/p0213 -yrbs.html#print.
3. Matthew 7:7.
4. John 8:32.
5. Psalm 126:5.
6. Matthew 5:4.
7. John 16:33, NIV.
8. See Psalm 34:18.

CHAPTER 13: DEALING WITH STUBBORN KNOTS

1. "Endocrine System," Cleveland Clinic, May 12, 2020, https://my.clevelandclinic.org/health/articles/21201 -endocrine-system#:~:text=The%20hormones%20created %20and%20released.
2. Blaise Pascal, *Pensées* (Mineola, N.Y.: Dover, 2003); see also Blaise Pascal, "Section II: The Misery of Man Without God," trans. W. F. Trotter, *Pensées,* www.leaderu.com/ cyber/books/pensees/pensees-SECTION-2.html.
3. Linda Stone, "Beyond Simple Multi-Tasking: Continuous Partial Attention," LindaStone.net, November 30, 2009, https://lindastone.net/2009/11/30/beyond-simple-multi -tasking-continuous-partial-attention. I first came across this concept in Brian Mackenzie, Andy Galpin, and Phil White's book *Unplugged: Evolve from Technology to Up-*

grade Your Fitness, Performance, and Consciousness (Las Vegas: Victory Belt, 2017), 83.

4. Eva Selhub, "Nutritional Psychiatry: Your Brain on Food," Harvard Health Publishing, September 18, 2022, www.health.harvard.edu/blog/nutritional-psychiatry-your-brain-on-food-201511168626.

5. Yuri Elkaim, "The Truth About How Much Water you Should Really Drink," *U.S. News and World Report*, September 13, 2013, https://health.usnews.com/health-news/blogs/eat-run/2013/09/13/the-truth-about-how-much-water-you-should-really-drink.

6. Linda Searing, "The Big Number: The Average U.S. Adult Sits 6.5 Hours a Day. For Teens, It's Even More," *The Washington Post*, April 28, 2019, www.washingtonpost.com/national/health-science/the-big-numberthe-average-us-adult-sits-65-hours-a-day-for-teens-its-even-more/2019/04/26/7c29e4c2-676a-11e9-a1b6-b29b90efa879_story.html.

7. John Anderer, "Even a Few Minutes of Daily Light Exercise Can Lower Depression Risk," StudyFinds, July 12, 2023, https://studyfinds.org/few-minutes-exercise-depression.

CHAPTER 14: FREE TO FEEL

1. Eugene H. Peterson, *Run with the Horses: The Quest for Life at Its Best* (Downers Grove, Ill.: InterVarsity, 2019), 148.

2. See Romans 7:15.

3. Psalm 91:1–4, NIV.

4. "The Serenity Prayer and Me," Alcoholics Anonymous, www.alcoholics-anonymous.org.uk/Members/Fellowship-Magazines/SHARE-Magazine/December-2019/The-Serenity-Prayer-and-Me.

5. Ecclesiastes 3:1–8.
6. For more on this topic, get a copy of Curt Thompson's book *The Soul of Desire: Discovering the Neuroscience of Longing, Beauty, and Community* (Downers Grove, Ill.: InterVarsity, 2021).

GO DEEPER WITH THE COMPANION VIDEO STUDY

Learn more about Jennie's Bible studies at
HarperChristianResources.com

Did you enjoy reading *Untangle Your Emotions*?

Check out these other bestsellers by Jennie Allen

FOR WHEN YOU FEEL *exhausted*

FOR WHEN YOU FEEL *overwhelmed*

FOR WHEN YOU FEEL *lonely*

LEARN MORE AT JENNIEALLEN.COM

LISTEN TO JENNIE'S PODCAST

MADE FOR THIS

IF:GATHERING

How do we reach an entire generation so that every single person knows Jesus?

Through you.

Jennie founded IF:Gathering in response to a phrase God continually laid on her heart: *disciple a generation.* Since 2014, IF:Gathering has been creating resources and hosting events to equip believers to learn more about who God is and disciple others right where they are.

To learn how you can be a part of discipling a generation, visit:

DiscipleAGeneration.com